Truth and the
ethics of criticism

In memory of E. P. Thompson

Truth and the ethics of criticism

Christopher Norris

Manchester University Press
Manchester and New York
Distributed exclusively in the USA and Canada by St Martin's Press

Copyright © Christopher Norris 1994

Published by Manchester University Press
Oxford Road, Manchester M13 9NR, UK
and Room 400, 175 Fifth Avenue, New York, NY 10010, USA

Distributed exclusively in the USA and Canada
by St. Martin's Press, Inc., 175 Fifth Avenue, New York,
NY 10010, USA

British Library Cataloguing-in-Publication Data
A catalogue record for this book is available from the British Library

Library of Congress Cataloging-in-Publication Data
Norris, Christopher,
    For truth in criticism / Christopher Norris.
      p.   cm.
    Includes bibliographical references and index.
    ISBN 0–7190–4452–9. — ISBN 0–7190–4453–7 (pbk)
    1. Critical theory. 2. Postmodernism. 3. Meaning (Philosophy)
    4. Meaninglessness (Philosophy)   I. Title.
B809.3.N67   1994
190'.9'04—dc20   94–16682
                                           CIP

ISBN 0 7190 4452 9 *hardback*
     0 7190 4453 7 *paperback*

Photoset in Linotron Sabon
by Northern Phototypesetting Co. Ltd, Bolton

Printed in Great Britain
by Bell & Bain Ltd, Glasgow

Contents

Acknowledgements

Once again I am grateful to my friends and graduate students in Cardiff for their willingness to read draft versions of this book and to criticize various points of argument and detail. Let me thank especially Taieb Belghazi, Clive Cazeaux, Ed Dascher, Gary Day, Kathy Kerr, Kevin Mills, Paul Norcross, Marianna Papastephanou, Lynn Reynolds, David Roden, and Shiva Srinivasan. The final version owes a lot to Christa Knellwolf – now at the University of Zürich – who offered encouragement and intellectual stimulus as the work went along. I was fortunate in teaching a joint course on aesthetics and critical theory with two of my colleagues – Andrew Edgar and Peter Sedgwick – whose ideas did much to sharpen my own understanding of the issues involved. Alessandra Tanesini will most likely disagree with just about everything in the book but will not, I hope, object too strongly if I inscribe her among the allies of enlightenment. Thanks also to Robin Attfield, Andrew Belsey, Michael Durrant, Suzanne Gibson, Stephen Møller, and Barry Wilkins for easing my *rite de passage* into the philosophy section at Cardiff; to my comrades in Côr Cochion, Caerdydd for their friendship and sustaining enthusiasm; to Reg Coates and Viv Deacon, *i migliori fabbri*; and to David Skilton for his support and generosity over the past few years. Siri Meyer invited me to Bergen (Norway) for a series of seminars on postmodernism, deconstruction and cultural politics which helped to focus my thought during the last stages of revision. All the same it is truer in this case than in most that any faults here remaining are mine alone. Certainly I can't blame them on Alison, Clare or Jenny, all of whom suffered the travails of authorship with a goodwilled tolerance far beyond the call of duty.

Cardiff, January 1994

Notes

Since this is a relatively short text it seemed best to number the notes and references in one continuous series rather than start a new sequence for each of its eleven sections. Readers should find this format more convenient ('user-friendly' in the current jargon) when referring back and forth between text and notes.

Some portions of this book have appeared as articles in the journals *Common Knowledge*, *The Southern Review*, and *Southern Humanities Review*. I am grateful to the editors and publishers concerned for permission to reprint this material in modified form.

I

Introduction: the retreat from high theory

A sociologist of culture could probably come up with some interesting facts – even statistics – about the spread of 'postmodernist' thinking in relation to localized differences of history, class-politics, economic development and so forth. This project might discover quite a range of home-truths with regard to the vagaries of intellectual fashion (especially in university departments of literature) and their wider cultural or socio-political context. Most revealing would be the inverse relation that arguably exists between the scope for off-campus political involvement – for various forms of 'grass-roots' activist concern – and the extent to which academics have embraced the current postmodernist turn.[1] For it is tempting to speculate that few would adopt this outlook of disabused *fin-de-siècle* wisdom were it not for their willing or enforced isolation in enclaves utterly remote from any contact with realities outside the seminar-room. Small wonder that it has produced such an array of exotic, hypercultivated hot-house blooms as a result of these adverse external conditions.

Nor is it in any way surprising that some of the most 'radical' attempts to deconstruct the very bases of Marxist or socialist thought (e.g. the categories of class, ideology, experience, purposive action etc.) have issued from 'post-Marxist' thinkers located in high-powered centres for 'theory' which have somehow sprung up in the very heartland of British conservatism.[2] No doubt such ideas have a certain heady appeal if life outside – as viewed (say) from the Essex University campus – offers such an unrelievedly bleak panorama. One is put in mind of Derrida's whimsical remark *à propos* the topography at Cornell: that the 'principle of reason' may likewise be suspended over the abyss (or *Abgrund*) that opens up beneath that precarious vantage-point.[3]

One might look to Perry Anderson's *Considerations on Western Marxism* (1977) for an early diagnosis of this widening rift between the politics of theory and the prospects for any kind of real-world practical engagement.[4] Even so one thinks back, if not with a keen Wordsworthian nostalgia ('bliss was it in that dawn to be alive!'), then at least with a sense that we have now moved on into some kind of eerie cultural twilight. For despite what Anderson noted as the rarefied level of debate – the seeming reversal of Marx's dictum that philosophers, having so long interpreted the world, should now at last be seeking to change it – there were undeniably some serious contenders around, among them Frankfurt-School critical theory, Althusserian Marxism, and Sartre's massively ambitious attempt to synthesize the projects of Marxist, existentialist, and psychoanalytic thought.[5] Of course these issues are still very much alive for anyone whose purview extends beyond the range of currently fashionable options. But so far as literary theorists are concerned they rate nothing more than the passing tribute of a sigh, or a footnote reference to that bygone era – twenty years back – when the talk was still of truth, critique, ideology, and suchlike delusive 'enlightenment' beliefs.

For many of my own generation (or those not suffering from selective amnesia) the stages of this process can be charted in relation to a series of conferences on the sociology of literature held during the late 1970s and early 80s on that same Essex University campus.[6] Here it was that successive new waves of Continental theory – from structuralism to post-structuralism and beyond – were registered each year with an almost seismographic sensitivity. Hence the crisis-laden rhetoric that so often marked these occasions, as one paradigm (or 'discourse') yielded to another, and as old certitudes were reluctantly abandoned when they turned out to rest on theoretical assumptions which the latest wisdom called into doubt. In short, all the signs were already pointing towards the advent of our present, much-touted 'postmodern condition', an epoch when – so the argument runs – we have at last managed to break with all those fraudulent 'meta-narratives' of progress, enlightenment, and truth at the end of enquiry.

Thus Althusserian Marxism problematized the notions of purposive agency, historical knowledge, class-consciousness, revolutionary praxis etc., only to be overtaken in turn by a

Foucauldian (Nietzsche-derived) rhetoric of 'power/knowledge' that left no room for Althusser's residual Marxist ideas of critique, ideology, and 'theoretical practice'.[8] And as post-structuralism set about critiquing its own (i.e. structuralist) precursor movement, so the course of real-world political events – in Britain, the United States, Eastern Europe and elsewhere – seemed ever more remote from anything envisaged by thinkers of a Marxist or left-liberal persuasion. It is easy to dismiss those old 'crises' of theory as so many storms-in-a-teacup, the products of a self-indulgent academic fondness for blowing up minor professional wrangles into events of epochal significance. But Althusser was right about this much at least: that theoretical disputes, no matter how arcane or specialized, are often the ground on which subjects articulate their own (doubtless 'overdetermined') relation to the real-world conflicts of knowledge and interest that define the present horizons of political possibility.[9] The retreat from such ideas – roughly speaking, the trajectory that led from Foucault to Lyotard, Baudrillard and the apostles of postmodernity – went along with a growing scepticism with regard to every last precept and principle of enlightenment critique. As reality dissolved into the structures of discursive or textual representation, so the subject (after Lacan: the 'subject-presumed-to-know') became just a locus of multiple shifting and transient subject-positions, or a specular reflex of the epistemic will-to-truth whose ubiquitous workings Foucault set out to expose. And from here it was no great distance to that stance of out-and-out cognitive scepticism – joined to an ultra-relativist position on issues of ethico-political judgment – which forms such a prominent (and depressing) feature of the current postmdernist cultural scene.[10]

What one chiefly recollects from the last couple of Essex conferences is the agonized debate as to whether there existed any further role for 'theory' if indeed it was the case that discourse, textuality, or representation went all the way down, and moreover – following Foucault – that theoretical truth-claims were inextricably linked to the covert operations of instituted power/knowledge. For it would then be the merest of illusions – a classic example of presumptuous vanguard intellectualism – to suppose that theorists had any right to speak out on matters of truth or justice that exceeded their competence in this or that field of specialized scholarly enquiry. Least of all could they claim – like so many before them in the (now superannuated) Kantian or Marxist traditions – to be somehow capable of theorizing the difference between truth and falsehood, knowledge and opinion, or justified (legitimate) ethico-political values and those which merely passed as such according to the currency of in-place consensus belief.[11] That these distinctions will nowadays strike many readers as possessing such a quaintly moralistic – not to say authoritarian – ring is one measure of the distance we have travelled down the road that Richard Rorty approvingly labels 'North Atlantic postmodern bourgeois liberal pragmatism'.[12] It is a route that branched off from anything meriting the name 'critical theory' at precisely the point where post-structuralism and its allied movements promoted the linguistic (or textualist) turn into a kind of wholesale negative ontology. This opened the way for a postmodern ethos that counted the world well lost for the sake of romping more freely in the hyperreal aftermath. For in truth there is little difference – bar the rhetoric – between postmodernism in its full-blown 'end-of-ideology' or 'end-of-history' guise and those varieties of *au courant* 'post-Marxist' (likewise 'post-feminist', etc.) thinking which blithely abandon all the arguments and values required of any critical project worthy the name.

II

Science, ideology, and 'local knowledge'

One lesson of all this – to resume my opening remarks – is that a great deal depends on where one happens to be in terms of the wider socio-political culture and the local opportunities for linking theory and practice in a meaningful way. Not that I would wish to be taken as endorsing any version of the crassly reductive view advanced by some sociologists of knowledge or sceptical debunkers in the post-modern–pragmatist vein. On this account 'local knowledge' is the most that we can ever hope for, since theoretical truth-claims amount to nothing more than the expression of in-place consensus beliefs on the part of some existing cultural enterprise, professional interest-group, 'interpretive community', or whatever. Such ideas have gained ground across a range of disciplines, influenced on the one hand by ethnographers and social anthropologists like Clifford Geertz, and on the other by various prevalent forms of deep-laid ontological and epistemological scepticism.[13] Among them one could instance the relativist drift in philosophy of science given its most influential formulation by Thomas Kuhn and pushed to the giddy (anarchist) limit by Paul Feyerabend; the 'linguistic turn' in its numerous (e.g. Wittgensteinian, hermeneutic, post-structuralist, Foucauldian and neo-pragmatist) forms; the wholesale rejection of 'foundationalist' thinking by philosophers of otherwise varied persuasion; and the widespread sense of a crisis (or a terminal breakdown) in the project of enlightenment thought, or what Habermas – chief among its latterday defenders – describes as the 'philosophic discourse of modernity'.[14] Of course there are important differences between and within these movements of thought. Nor, for that matter, could it seriously be maintained that there exists only a difference of emphasis or rhetorical idiom between (say)

Quine's arguments on the topic of 'ontological relativity' and those forms of *de rigueur* ultra-relativist doctrine that currently occupy the high ground of cultural fashion.[15] But these have often been lumped together by literary theorists – as indeed by 'post-philosophical' thinkers like Rorty – as so many signals that we have now moved on to a stage in the 'cultural conversation' where the old talking-points (truth, reason, reality etc.) have simply lost whatever interest or relevance they once seemed to possess. In which case clearly one could make little headway by arguing for a different kind of 'local knowledge', one that took strength from its own, more propitious circumstances, but which still came down to a pragmatist conception of truth as locally and contingently warranted belief.

One purpose of this essay is to demarcate these various approach-routes to our so-called 'postmodern condition' and thereby provide – as I hope – a more critical perspective on the issues involved. Another is to challenge the current post-structuralist *doxa* that would treat (for instance) Althusserian Marxism or Derridean deconstruction as so many stages – or specialized detours – on the path to its own thoroughgoing form of cultural and linguistic relativism. What drops out of sight in such accounts, premised as they are on the absolute centrality of Saussure's theoretical 'revolution', is the complex and distinctive philosophical pre-history which informed those projects from the outset. For it is well to be reminded, despite and against the current wisdom, that the truth or theoretical adequacy of an argument cannot be measured solely in terms of what is 'good in the way of belief'. I count myself fortunate in having been a student at University College, London at the time of Frank Kermode's graduate seminars when the new French thinking – Lacan, Althusser, Derrida, Barthes – had not yet hardened into an ironcast orthodoxy with punitive sanctions attached. And life in Cardiff (where I have taught for the past fifteen years) has the signal advantage that the real world still exists within hailing distance for those not altogether sold on talk of reality as a textual construct or of subject-positions as constituted always in and through 'discourse'. To put it bluntly: there is less excuse for being a postmodernist in Cardiff than in other places where the new solipsism exerts an understandable (though none the less regressive and politically enervating) appeal.

One very active source of confusion is the fallacy that moves from a reasonable premise – that local interests often decide what counts as a worthwhile, productive, or interesting line of thought – to the relativist conclusion that 'truth' *just is* the complimentary label we standardly attach to whatever fits in with those interests. Thus for instance it is clearly the case that Western science might conceivably have taken a quite different direction at some decisive point in its history. Or again – as we learn from Joseph Needham's magisterial account of Chinese science and civilization – another culture might have set out even earlier along the same path of technological discovery, and then for some reason lost interest and adopted a wholly divergent set of social aims and priorities.[16] So to this extent the relativists are right: that scientific theories and truth-claims always take rise within some given (culture-specific) history of human endeavour, or as the upshot of practices – research-programmes, investigative paradigms etc. – which likewise belong to their own time and place. But this is not to say that any items of knowledge thus acquired possess truth or validity only with reference to that same background of localized cultural interests. Nor can it be taken as a knock-down argument for the kind of wholesale relativist outlook which asserts that truth is just a matter of our present and contingent ideas of what is 'good in the way of belief'. It is one thing to hold that the findings of recent research into microphysics or aerodynamics wouldn't make any sense in a culture that had no use for computers, radar technology, brain-scan instruments, rapid air transport, and other such perquisites of the late twentieth-century Western life-world. But it is quite a different thing to maintain – with thinkers like Rorty and Paul Feyerabend – that these are just so many spin-off products of an optional language-game that figures the world according to its own temporarily favoured models or metaphors.[17] One is tempted to suggest that such an argument could seem persuasive only to those who write it out on their laptop machines at thirty thousand feet while remaining largely ignorant of whatever it is that prevents both technologies from crashing.

No doubt there are cultures – past, present, or possible worlds – in which most of what we take for granted as scientific fact would appear either useless or wildly implausible. Then again, one could argue (as relativists often do) that history to date offers so many cases of well-entrenched scientific truth-claims turning out to be false, partial, or of limited application that nobody with a decent working knowledge of that history could nowadays wish to defend any version of the realist, constructive or problem-solving paradigm.

Much better abandon that old Enlightenment discourse and accept that truth is indeed just a product of our localized knowledge-constitutive interests, or an honorific name for those beliefs that currently hold the field. Such ideas are common coin among cultural and literary theorists, not least – one suspects – because they have laboured so long under a sense of disadvantage as compared with the scientists, philosophers, and other claimants to an order of truth that transcends mere rhetoric or opinion (*doxa*) in the quest for genuine knowledge (*episteme*). After all those magisterial put-downs, from Plato to the logical positivists, it is perhaps small wonder that thinkers in the humanities should make a bid for whatever suits their purpose in the way of 'advanced' (i.e. sceptical or ultra-relativist) philosophy of science. From here, so it seems, the path is wide open to a turning of the tables that would – in vulgar-deconstructionist fashion – treat all concepts as metaphors, all truth-claims as so many operative fictions, and all 'discourse' (scientific discourse included) as merely the product of this or that optional interpretative paradigm. And with philosophers like Rorty and Feyerabend around, this viewpoint is not lacking for notional support from the other side of the fence.

So literary theorists have a lot to gain, at least in terms of their elective self-image, from an approach that claims to cut science down to size. This approach would stress its character as 'local knowledge', its sociological determinants, its adoption of various 'textual' models and metaphors, or its role as just one – strictly non-privileged – voice in the ongoing 'cultural coversation of mankind'. In fact they (the literary theorists) are admirably placed to reveal all this on account of their own acquired expertise in the discovery of latent figural, narrative, or tropological structures in every kind of text. Hence – as Paisley Livingston notes in his book *Literary Knowledge* – their penchant for speculative themes from the new physics (undecidability, complementarity, ontological relativity, the wave/particle dualism) whose appeal derives mainly from this promise of somehow levelling the field between science and the 'soft', i.e., interpretative or hermeneutic disciplines.[18] Hence also the current high vogue for chaos theory among literary intellectuals who tend to invoke it, most often, as yet further back-up for their postmodern line as regards the obsolescence of truth, reason, enlightenment 'grand narratives', and so forth. Lyotard offers a fair sample when he gestures towards that dimension of scientific thinking which, 'by concerning itself with such things as undecidables, the limits of precise control, conflicts characterized by incomplete information, '*fracta*', catastrophes, and pragmatic paradoxes . . . is theorizing its own evolution as discontinuous, catastrophic, non-rectifiable and paradoxical'.[20]

The strong whiff of mystery-mongering here is reinforced by the parallel with contemporary theologians who take comfort from any hint that science has to acknowledge limits to its present powers of explanatory grasp. In fact the honourable term 'sceptic' is wholly misapplied to a thinker such as Feyerabend who would champion Cardinal Bellarmine and the Church authorities against the upstart heretic Galileo, or to those who – following Rorty – regard the issue between them as merely a matter of alternative metaphors, one of which (the heliocentric model) just happens to have won out and thus set the agenda for subsequent 'scientific' thought.[20] That these ideas enjoy widespread popularity among cultural theorists is more a symptom of their scientific ignorance – or of the current state of play in inter-departmental politics – than a sign that we have now matured, as Rorty would have it, into an attitude of healthy scepticism *vis-à-vis* the grandiose delusions of an earlier time.

Not that such interdisciplinary overtures are always or necessarily bound up with this desire to knock science off its pedestal. They go back to the heroic period of Cambridge physics during the 1920s when literary critics – I. A. Richards and William Empson among them – were keen to build bridges between what other commentators were already starting to think of as the 'two cultures'. In Richards's case, one might argue, this liaison had unfortunate consequences. For it led him at first to adopt the narrowly scientistic view that truth-claims in poetry could be only a species of 'emotive' utterance or 'pseudo-statement', failing as they did on both logical-positivist counts, i.e. when assessed as factual propositions borne out by empirical testing or as analytic truths self-evident to reason by virtue of their logical form.[21] Later on – influenced by his reading of Niels Bohr and the philosophy of quantum mechanics – Richards abandoned this dead-end perspective and embraced a more sophisticated view of the relation between language, logic, and truth.[22] With Empson such reflections are already well advanced in his first book *Seven Types of Ambiguity* (1930) and in the poetry of his Cambridge undergraduate years when Empson – on his own retrospective account – was deliberately 'imitating Donne' in the attempt to make 'human and imaginative sense' of the scientific theories current at the time.[23] These interests were obliquely carried forward into *The Structure of Complex Words* (1951), a book whose dogged yet subtle defence of a rationalist philosophy of mind and a truth-conditional semantics as applied to literary language were so much at odds with the prevailing wisdom that it remains one of the great neglected works of recent critical theory.[24] My point here is simply to bring out the contrast between Empson's speculative but deeply informed engagement with science and the current style of know-all, know-nothing 'theory' that exploits such analogies only for the sake of their presumed ultra-relativist upshot. For the idea has got around that if science can be shown to partake of the postmodern or 'textualist' condition, then realist ontologies are hopelessly *dépassé* along with all talk of reason, truth, critique, and suchlike delusive 'enlightenment' notions. In which case – so the argument tacitly runs – we are better off trusting to those (i.e. the postmodernists, neo-pragmatists, textualists of various persuasion) who count reality a poor thing in comparison with this new-found realm of open-ended hermeneutic freedom.

One source of such thinking is the idea (often derived from a cursory acquaintance with Derrida's texts) that since metaphor pervades the language of science and philosophy, therefore it follows that no truth is to be had beyond the endless chain of linguistic *différance*, or the constant process of displacement from one paradigm ('discourse', 'conceptual scheme' etc.) to the next. That this reading is erroneous – a flat misconstrual of Derrida's essay 'White Mythology' – is a case that I have argued at length elsewhere.[25] It ignores, among other things, his repeated insistence that we cannot make sense of the term 'metaphor' – let alone theorize its workings, its relation to 'literal' usage, its problematic role within the texts of philosophy, etc. – except by engaging those texts with *at least* the same degree of analytical precision that philosophers have hitherto brought to that task. Thus there is no point saying, with breezy assurance, that 'all concepts are metaphors' (all truth-claims rhetorical, all philosophy just a 'kind of writing' and so forth) if one thereby deprives criticism of the analytic means – the conceptual resources – required to make good such an argument. It is the same point that Derrida raises against Foucault with regard to certain passages in the latter's book *Madness and Civilization*.[26] Here again there is a self-disabling paradox – a 'performative contradiction', to adopt the Habermasian term – in Foucault's strictly exorbitant claim to be somehow speaking from a position outside the very discourse of Western (post-Cartesian) reason on behalf of those oppressed or deviant voices which that discourse has sedulously kept off bounds. Foucault cannot advance a single proposition – let alone a whole book of inter-articulated statements, judgments, inferences, and truth-claims – without necessarily falling back into the forms of rational argumentation. Had Habermas taken the point of this essay (and of 'White Mythology' likewise) then he might not have placed Derrida so squarely in the company of Foucault, Lyotard, and other 'young conservative' or counter-enlightenment enemies of reason.[27] What sets Derrida's thinking apart from theirs is a constant (and lately more explicit) awareness of the need to keep faith with the 'unfinished project of modernity', even while continuing to criticize that project for its blind-spots of unexamined prejudice.

I hope that this will go some way towards resolving the apparent contradiction in my argument so far. That is to say, I have contended on the one hand that truth in these matters is not just a product of localized language-games, conventions, socio-political priorities, cultural 'forms of life' and so forth. Yet I have also argued – with a glance at the shifting currency of recent debate – that circumstances may be more or less propitious for the kinds of genuinely critical endeavour that keep such interests and values in view. In fact this is not so much a genuine dilemma as a pseudo-problem that arises only when scepticism of a wholesale (postmodern) variety has already taken hold. Thus, for thinkers like Lyotard, 'truth' is conceived as an absolute, timeless, monological discourse whose effect is to suppress the narrative 'differend' and thus to commit an ethico-discursive wrong against anyone who fails to accept its criteria or acknowledge its veridical status.[28] Rather we should seek to maximize the narrative differentials – the range of 'first-order natural pragmatic' story-telling modes – and henceforth reject any language-game (or 'phrase-regime') that would claim a monopoly of truth, reason, or virtue. This is fine up to a point, i.e. in so far as it encourages an outlook of tolerant respect for the variety of human values. On this reading it is pretty much in line with the enlightenment critique of revelation and with the secularizing impulse that has long held out against doctrinal impositions in the name of this or that trans-cendent, self-authorizing creed. But postmodernists typically con-fuse the issue by ignoring the difference – the crucial difference –

between 'truth' as a matter of privileged access, vouchsafed to some religious or secular elite already (so to speak) 'in the know', and truth as arrived at through reasoned enquiry in the public sphere of open participant debate. In so doing – as Habermas justly remarks – they revert to a pre-enlightenment ethos when faith (not reason) was the arbiter of right thinking, and when the 'hermeneutic circle' (so beloved of present-day theorists) indeed marked the horizon of permissible belief.[29]

This may seem an odd charge to bring in view of Lyotard's pluralist rhetoric, his stress on the open multiplicity of language-games, each disposing of its own immanent criteria and none having the right to adjudicate over any other. But the effect of this incommensurability-thesis – derived from a mixture of post-structuralist, Wittgensteinian and liberal-communitarian ideas – is to render criticism pretty much otiose in the face of practices or beliefs (no matter how obnoxious) which subscribe to some different language-game or set of cultural norms. In fact there is little to choose, preferential idioms aside, between Rorty's pragmatist talk of consensus as the aim of civilized debate (treating truth as just a matter of what's currently and contingently 'good in the way of belief') and Lyotard's proposal that we should strive to maximize 'dissensus' as a means of furthering the interests of justice in a liberal-pluralist polity. For they are agreed on the following points: (1) that the Enlightenment project (or the philosophic discourse of modernity) has entered a phase of terminal decline; (2) that any attempt to revive that project is sure to have bad (ethically and politically retrograde) effects; and (3) that since 'critique' in the old (e.g. Kantian or Marxist) sense has now gone the way of all those other outmoded 'meta-narrative' concepts, therefore the best – indeed the only – alternative is an ongoing 'cultural conversation' which acknowledges its own strictly localized character and abjures any thought of truth and validity beyond its immediate sphere. Only thus, according to Lyotard, can a *certain idea* of Enlightenment – standardly equated with Western notions of reason, progress, political 'maturity' etc. – be prevented from continuing to impose its culture-specific norms under cover of a universalist rhetoric which easily translates into forms of cultural imperialism.

However, this argument comes unstuck at the point where one asks what *reason* any liberal-minded Westerner could have for giving up the (doubtless ethnocentric) belief that on balance theirs is the best of all hitherto- and currently-existing worlds. At least this Rortian position has the merit of obliging him – unlike Lyotard – to grasp the dilemma by one of its horns and declare himself frankly 'ethnocentric' in the sense of having no choice but to speak from a standpoint ('North Atlantic postmodern bourgeois liberal pragmatist') that defines his self-image as reflected by the language-game currently and locally on offer. For there is simply no alternative, as Rorty sees it, no standpoint from which one might compare and criticize the various options, or again, no 'skyhook' from which to hang the arguments for a radically different mode of thought. Elsewhere – in more sanguine moments – he inclines to make a virtue of necessity by remarking that liberal democracy, US-style, is anyway the best thing that humankind has yet come up with on its long trek towards freedom, justice, and equality. One can readily concede his entitlement to this view, which of course has to be judged on its merits, i.e. in the light of US domestic and foreign policy, of existing differentials between wealth and poverty, private affluence and public squalor, the feel-good rhetoric of 'freedom' and 'democracy' as opposed to the realities of urban deprivation, overseas wars, the undermining of democratically elected socialist regimes in Latin America, and so forth. That is to say, any adequate counter-argument will need to produce both factual and principled reasons for thinking Rorty's position naive, misinformed, or (at the very least) ideologically motivated.[31] But it is just such arguments that Rorty excludes *a priori* by counting it strictly impossible – a Houdini-like illusionist trick – that thinking should criticize the in-place beliefs, the cultural norms or political values of its own place and time. No doubt (and here again he is on a wavelength with Lyotard) there is room for quite a measure of internal 'dissensus' within any given community. But in the end such differences only make sense – only register as part of a meaningful dialogue – on condition that all parties subscribe to the wider conversational rules of the game.

According to Rorty pragmatism is the end of the road that just about every notable thinker has been travelling for the past fifty years and more. In various forms – hermeneutic, post-structuralist, post-analytic, liberal-communitarian etc. – it is a *terminus ad quem* that always beckons at the point where thinking comes up against the fact of its own culturally-situated character. On this view one can take a motley assortment of philosophers and treat them all as more or less

willing converts to the pragmatist persuasion. Thus Hegel is subjected to a 'naturalized' reading that junks his ideas of *Aufhebung*,
dialectical progress, Absolute Reason, and so forth, and values what
is left for its straightforward story-telling interest.[32] Heidegger
would likewise have turned out a good pragmatist had he only
relinquished his aversion to all things American (pragmatism
included) and given up all that pointless talk about 'Being' and
'ontological difference'.[33] Foucault could have got there easily
enough if he had thought a bit less about 'power/knowledge',
genealogy, 'micropolitics' and suchlike notions, and pushed right
through with his promising line on the aesthetics of private self-
fashioning.[34] And in the analytic camp there are thinkers like Quine
and Davidson who can always be nudged in the same direction by a
reading that tactfully ignores their moments of retrograde (truth-
fixated) talk, and which coaxes them down to a sensible acceptance
of the pragmatist or holist viewpoint.[35]

This is not the place for a detailed critique of the various strategies
that Rorty deploys in thus reducing the entirety of present-day
thought to so many roundabout variations on the end-of-philosophy
theme. My point is rather to locate the odd conjunction of a post-
modern-pluralist rhetoric – one that professedly holds out a welcome to the widest variety of language-games, discourses, cultural
forms of life, etc. – with an outlook which in fact, if consistently
maintained, would deny us any access to belief-systems other than
our own. Consider the following sequence of arguments, each of
them derivable from Rorty's or Lyotard's version of the language-
game doctrine. (1) All truth-talk is henceforth to be construed as
relative to this or that contingent cultural practice. (2) We can make
sense of such practices only in so far as we share the relevant beliefs,
values, attitudes, or criteria for meaningful utterance. (3) It is wrong
– an infraction of the speech-act or narrative 'differend' – to assess
other language-games by our own (likewise relative) cultural lights.
But (4) we are always doing just that since really we have no choice in
the matter. That is to say that (5) there is simply no escaping the
hermeneutic circle – the interpretive horizon of pre-given beliefs,
criteria, sense-making strategies, and so forth – which we apply
willy-nilly in seeking to understand beliefs other than our own. In
which case (6) we might as well admit that the relativist formula 'true
in L' (i.e., 'valid according to the norms of some other, perhaps quite
alien language-game or cultural form of life') will always carry the

inbuilt rider: ' "true in L" for all that we can possibly know, but only comprehensible to us when translated into locally familiar terms'. And clearly it will make a lot of difference – not least to those whose beliefs are being thus construed – when the terms in question happen to belong to a culture that wields considerable power in the shaping of global power-relations.

This point about the limits of relativist thinking can be made in various ways. Some philosophers – Donald Davidson and Hilary Putnam among them – have responded with a form of the Kantian 'conditions of possibility' argument, in this case designed to bring out the kinds of self-disabling paradox (or performative contradiction) to which such ideas fall prey. Hence Putnam's demonstration, *contra* Rorty, that what starts out as an attitude of easygoing tolerance for the range of human cultures, lifestyles or 'final vocabularies' may yet end up by adopting a stance of likewise genial but none the less deep-laid ethnocentrism.[36] Davidson pursues a related line of argument in his well-known essay 'On the Very Idea of a Conceptual Scheme'.[37] Taking issue with a range of otherwise diverse positions – from Quine on the topic of 'ontological relativity' to the ethno-linguistics of B. L. Whorf and the ideas advanced by philosophers of science like Kuhn and Feyerabend – he contends that their arguments would make no sense were it not for the fact that we can and do translate (successfully for the most part) between different world-views, paradigms, discourses, cultural forms of life, and so forth. Thus: 'Whorf, wanting to demonstrate that Hopi incorporates a metaphysics so alien to ours that Hopi and English cannot, as he puts it, "be calibrated", uses English to convey the content of sample Hopi sentences.'[38] And again, as against Quine: '[t]here does not seem to be much hope for a test that a conceptual scheme is radically different from ours if that test depends on the assumption that we can divorce the notion of truth from that of translation'.[39]

What this amounts to is a version of the 'transcendental *tu quoque*' that Habermas deploys to similar effect against postmodern sceptics like Foucault and Lyotard. For without the possibility of right understanding – of truth (or valid inference) as the precondition for any communicative act – we should have no means to recognize cases where understanding had indeed broken down, or where translation came up against some genuine problem of localized interpretative grasp. Such recognition, in Davidson's words, 'may take the form of widespread sharing of sentences held true by speakers of "the same language", or agreement in the large mediated by a theory of truth contrived by an interpreter for speakers of another language'.[40] In either case it excludes the ultra-relativist thesis that we might be massively in error as regards the 'conceptual scheme' – the entire apparatus of truth-conditions, inferential procedures, ontological commitments etc. – that charac-terized the target language. For in this case (envisaged *per impossibile* in Quine's famous thought-experiment with the 'radical translator') we should start out by denying that it was in fact a 'language' in any sense of that term intelligible to us as language-using creatures.[41] That is to say, we should regard it as simply beyond the pale of discourse or communicative utterance, taking these to entail certain minimal attributes – reference, predication, values of truth and falsehood – in the absence of which no language could conceivably function. 'What forms the skeleton of what we call a language is the pattern of inference and structure created by the logical constants, the sentential connectives, quantifiers, and devices for cross-reference.'[42] Syntax is therefore, as Davidson puts it, more 'sociable' than semantics to the extent that it affords this improved prospect for securing communicative uptake.

This helps to explain what is wrong with the kinds of relativist argument typically derived from the 'linguistic turn' in its various present-day forms. Common to them all – post-structuralist, Foucauldian, neo-pragmatist, Wittgensteinian, etc. – is an ill-defined notion of 'language' that ignores or downplays the syntactic component (in Davidson's sense of that term), and which treats issues of meaning and truth from a narrowly semantic viewpoint. Hence the ease with which these theories move across from talk about 'language-games', discourses, 'final vocabularies' (Rorty), or the 'arbitrary' nature of the sign to talk about truth as wholly a product of cultural–linguistic convention. For Davidson, on the contrary, '[p]hilosophers who make convention a necessary element in language have the matter backward. The truth is rather that language is a condition for having conventions.'[43] And since lan-guage, in any adequate sense of that term, doesn't involve just words, signs or 'vocabularies' taken out of context, but also (more crucially) sentences, propositions, and higher-level forms of articulate discourse, it follows that conventionalist doctrines – along with their relativist progeny – need not carry the day.

What this amounts to is the claim, in Davidsonian terms, that 'a theory is better the more of its own resources it reads into the language for which it is a theory'.[44] And it can do so only by working on the 'principle of charity' which is not so much an option as a precondition for the theorist (or translator) who wants to make sense of that language. This principle assumes first that other speakers have an elementary interest (like us) in getting things right; second, that such rightness – taken 'in the large' – involves certain shared linguistic attributes; and third, that any problems of communication *on their side or ours* can best be sorted out by appeal to those features which make up the strictly ineliminable basis of all understanding within or between languages. For without such resources – and this is the crucial point – we should have no means either of comprehending others or of seeing where our own more parochial assumptions had previously led us astray.

Thus 'we compensate for the paucity of evidence concerning the meaning of individual sentences not by trying to produce evidence for the meanings of words but by considering the evidence for a theory of the language to which those words belong'.[45] On the relativist view such an argument is inherently deluded since it ignores the ever-present possibility that the language in question will share few or none of those 'resources' that the theorist brings to it. Thus the upshot will at best be a Quinean predicament of radical uncertainty (where the native informant's 'Gavagai!' might be taken to mean 'rabbit', 'undetached rabbit-part', 'nice to eat', 'saw one like it yesterday', or whatever) and at worst an inveterate cultural imperialism that reads its own 'resources' into everything and which makes no bones about the consequent dissymmetry of power-relations. But for Davidson this is once again to 'get the matter backward'. Like Putnam, he perceives a much greater risk – both of misunderstanding and of cultural imperialism in a subtler, more insidious form – entailed by those varieties of relativist thinking that in effect leave the interpreter with no choice but always to translate back into his or her 'language-game', 'discourse', or 'final vocabulary'. For if this were the case – if semantics indeed went all the way down – then interpretation would remain tightly sealed within the hermeneutic circle of its own linguistic horizon or conceptual scheme. On Davidson's account, conversely, it is by virtue of the 'principle of charity' that we can impute intelligible (truth-preserving) motives and meanings to speakers whose linguistic conventions are otherwise markedly at odds with our own.

Thus '[t]he methodological problem of interpretation is to see
how, given the sentences a man [sic] accepts as true under given
conditions, to work out what his beliefs are and what his words
mean'.[46] In which case nothing crucial is conceded – and certainly no
hostages yielded to the ultra-relativist case – if one acknowledges,
with Davidson, that 'sentences are true, and words refer, relative to a
language'. For this is just to say (as can hardly be denied) that
languages differ in all sorts of ways as regards their vocabularies,
their semantic fields, their range of adjectival (e.g. colour-term)
descriptions, and other such examples commonly cited by thinkers
of a relativist – nowadays chiefly post-structuralist – persuasion. But
Davidson's point still holds: that such differences can show up (or be
rendered intelligible) only on the basis of a shared commitment to
presupposed standards of truth, relevance, contextual implication,
and so forth. This is why, contrary to relativist claims, there is
nothing inherently 'oppressive' or 'monological' – much less any
kind of inbuilt cultural imperialism – about the argument from
shared standards of rationality and truth. To maintain this position is simply to acknowledge that we can best make sense of
unfamiliar languages, cultures, or beliefs – best do them justice – on
the assumption that any sticking-points encountered along the way
will most likely yield some ultimate agreement on the differences
involved.

This means in turn that 'whether we like it or not, if we want to
understand others, we must count them right on most matters'.[47] For
it follows from the principle of charity that when interpreting a
problematic utterance we must first try to establish the relevant
context of belief (of sentences held true by the speaker), and then
assign meanings in accordance with the truth of their belief-system
taken 'in the large'. To entertain the contrary hypothesis – to think in
terms of 'radical translation', of full-scale 'ontological relativity', of
incommensurable 'language-games' or 'conceptual schemes' – is to
give up any hope of establishing contact across localized differences
of view. 'If we can produce a theory that reconciles charity and the
formal conditions for a theory, we have done all that could be done
to ensure communication. Nothing more is possible, and nothing
more is needed.'[48] From the relativist standpoint, conversely, any
such theory would always be a construction out of our own pre-
given habits of thought and belief. Nor could its liberal-pluralist

credentials provide some guard against the imposition of those values through default of alternative resources. For in the absence of shared criteria we could no more recognize the other's claim to be 'right on most matters' than acknowledge the possibility of *our* being wrong on certain local points of interpretive dispute. And so it comes about – as Putnam remarks – that the relativist in fact winds up by tacitly denying the intelligibility of any language but his or her own.

III

Knowledge and human interests: Habermas, Lyotard, Foucault

I have allowed myself this lengthy detour via Davidson's arguments about truth and interpretation since they go to the heart of numerous present-day issues in critical theory, philosophy, and the human sciences. Most crucial is the question of how truth-claims can be redeemed in the face of a currently widespread retreat from the values and priorities of Enlightenment thought, or – in Habermas's resonant phrase – from the 'unfinished project of modernity'. It is for this reason that Habermas takes issue with Gadamer as regards the 'hermeneutic circle', the idea that understanding always and necessarily proceeds from within some pre-given horizon of interpretative values, beliefs, and expectations. Of course there is a sense – a trivial sense – in which Gadamer's claim must be true. That is to say, comprehension could never come about were it really the case (as in Quine's extravagant hypothesis) that it had to begin from scratch, through some act of 'radical translation', or on the basis of a crypto-analytic approach that abjured even the most minimal degree of shared ontological commitment. So it is useful to have Gadamer's reminder – as against such forms of hyperinduced sceptical doubt – that we possess a good deal more in the way of interpretative resources (or tacit 'preunderstanding') than is allowed for by artificial thought-experiments in the Quinean mode.[49] Quite simply we couldn't make a start in interpreting even the most basic utterances, whether of our own or any other language, if deprived (*per impossibile*) of everything that enters into the normal process of social and communicative exchange. In this sense the 'hermeneutic circle' is just a shorthand for that whole range of skills, knowledges, cultural codes, inferential reasonings, and so forth which make up our elementary competence as speakers and interpreters of language.

To adopt Quine's fiction of the 'radical translator' – along with its attendant doctrine of full-scale ontological relativity – is therefore to miss the most crucial point about the way human beings communicate.

But of course this argument can be turned right around by countering (as from a Quinean, post-structuralist, or Wittgensteinian 'language-games'/'forms-of-life' standpoint) that such competence is restricted to its own cultural sphere, and offers no assurance – much less any formal guarantee – that it holds for cases of inter-linguistic or cross-cultural exchange. One would then have little choice but to concede the relativist case, together with the yet more damaging concession (likewise invoking the 'hermeneutic circle') that we are always condemned to construe other people's meanings, intentions, beliefs, arguments, and truth-claims on terms laid down by our own pre-given habits of interpretative grasp. There could then be no question of adopting the Putnam–Davidson 'principle of charity', based as it is on the twofold assumption (1) that other people may have ideas very different from our own, but (2) that we can still make sense of those ideas – and register the fact of their difference – by recourse to certain deeper regularities in the nature of thought and language.

Hence Habermas's long-running quarrel with Gadamer, couched in the broadly 'Continental' idiom of hermeneutics, transcendental arguments, conditions of possibility, *Ideologiekritik* etc., but also bearing directly on these issues in the Anglo-American analytic sphere.[50] What Habermas objects to is not so much the notion of the 'hermeneutic circle' *per se* – the idea that understanding necessarily takes rise from some context of shared interpretative beliefs – but the way that this idea is so often recruited for extreme forms of cultural relativism and, by the same token, for conservative, consensus-based, or pragmatist doctrines of truth as (purely and simply) what is 'good in the way of belief'. Thus he argues against Gadamer that 'truth' so conceived may in fact be a product of *false* (systematically distorted) beliefs whose currency derives from their happening to fit with some dominant nexus of power/knowledge interests. Such agreement is 'pseudo-communicatively induced' – to adopt Habermas's grating terminology – in so far as it appears to be the upshot of free and open participant debate, while in fact allowing 'public opinion' to be massaged by those with the greatest measure of political influence, media access, or command of the relevant information-sources. What completely drops out is any prospect of distinguishing between this kind of in-place, *de facto* consensus and the shared human interest in achieving a *genuine* 'public sphere', a communicative forum no longer subject to the pressures of ideological coercion or manipulative thought-control.

It is not hard to see how this argument might apply to certain aspects of life in the present-day Western liberal pseudo-democracies. On the pragmatist account there is simply no difference – no difference that makes any difference – between truth as construed in relation to current societal or cultural norms and truth as the end-point of reasoned enquiry, as a Kantian 'regulative idea', or again (in Habermasian terms) through the appeal to an 'ideal speech-situation' redeemed from those various distorting pressures. Nor is this merely a technical issue, of concern only to critical theorists and philosophers of language. It is within reach of the larger question – central to the Enlightenment tradition of thought from Kant to Habermas – as to how far reason can legitimately claim to contest or to criticize what is currently held as 'good in the way of belief'. Such criticism may assume a wide variety of forms, from Marxist or other (e.g. left-liberal) versions of *Ideologiekritik* to philosophical projects aimed at defending the possibility of a critical-realist approach in the natural and human sciences. What unites them, I would suggest, is an argued and principled resistance to any version of the claim that truth comes down to a matter of local knowledge, consensus-values, or cultural forms of life.

This counter-argument can be set out very briefly as a series of propositions that bring together Davidson's 'principle of charity' (likewise his case against redundant or question-begging talk of 'conceptual schemes') with Habermas's theory of 'communicative action' or 'transcendental pragmatics'. (1) Issues of truth and falsehood are prior – logically and methodologically prior – to issues in the realm of semantic understanding, of cultural difference, or of depth-hermeneutics in the Gadamerian mode. (2) It is thus possible to criticize erroneous beliefs without thereby falling into the worse error (so construed by Gadamer, Wittgenstein, Winch, Lyotard *et al.*) of imposing one's own imperious beliefs on those whose criteria for meaningful expression differ so completely from ours as to place their utterances beyond reach of such criticism.[51] From which it follows (3) that argument doesn't have an end at the point of acknowledging diverse (incommensurable) language-games, paradigms, conceptual schemes, interpretive horizons, or whatever. On the contrary: (4) what enables us to perceive significant differences of view (or problems of linguistic grasp) is the presupposition that both parties have an interest – a knowledge-constitutive interest – in getting things right. And this entails the further axiom (5) that, in Davidson's laconic formulation, 'if we want to understand others, we must count them right on most matters'. Otherwise it would always be possible *either* (as Quine makes out) that we and they were operating on entirely different 'conceptual schemes', and were thus at cross-purposes from the start, *or* that both parties were massively in error with regard to some ultimate truth of the matter which – *ex hypothese* – neither could recognize. Whence the conclusion (6) that ontological relativism of this sort is strictly incoherent, along with any doctrine (including that of the 'hermeneutic circle') which relativizes truth to some particular language-game, discourse, or local interpretive horizon. For on this account it is not just our kind of 'truth' that drops out – as the relativists would cheerfully maintain – but also any prospect of revising or rejecting our own pre-existent beliefs in light of alternative truth-claims.

So there are, I would suggest, some worthwhile analogies to be drawn between Davidson's and Habermas's thinking, despite all their manifest disparities of style and background philosophical culture. Both put the case for conceiving of truth – or the orientation towards truth – as a starting-point and minimal precondition for any kind of interpretive enquiry. In Habermas this commitment takes the form of a reconstructive project designed to sustain the critical impulse of Enlightenment thought while taking account of the 'linguistic turn' and other such anti-foundationalist lines of argument. Hence the very marked change of emphasis that occurs between an early work like *Knowledge and Human Interests* (1968) and the discourse-ethics – or theory of communicative action – that Habermas has developed over the past two decades.[52] Simply stated, it is the shift from a Kantian (epistemological or subject-centred) paradigm to one that construes the various orders of judgment – cognitive, ethico-political, and aesthetic – with reference to inter-subjective norms of validity and good-faith dialogue. Of course there are large differences of view among his commentators as to the extent of this shift and its implications for Habermas's project as a whole. From a post-structuralist or postmodernist viewpoint it appears little more than a tactical ploy scarcely disguising his con-

tinued allegiance to that bad old Enlightenment discourse of reason
and truth. For Rorty, it is a kind of half-way house or shuffling
compromise position, one that continues to invoke those values
while conceding the linguistic (or the pragmatist) turn in all but
name. Then again there are those – myself included – who would
argue, on the contrary, that Habermas has yielded too much ground
in the face of this prevailing anti-foundationalist trend.[53] Hence the
plausibility of Rorty's claim that really there is no difference (bar the
rhetoric) between Habermas's talk of 'transcendental pragmatics',
'ideal speech-situations' etc. and the pragmatist outlook that levels
such talk to the currency of in-place consensus belief.

It could further be argued – as for instance by Onora O'Neill in her
recent book on Kantian ethics – that the charge of 'foundationalism'
is routinely misapplied by those (like Rorty or the liberal-
communitarians) who take it to denote a rock-bottom faith in the
truth-claims of epistemolgical enquiry quite apart from any wider
validating context of knowledge-constitutive values.[54] In so doing
they ignore those passages in the first *Critique* that make it clear how
far Kant is from endorsing such a view, and how firm his commitment – from the outset – to an understanding of the natural and
human sciences which regards the interests of truth-seeking thought
as always bound up with a tacit appeal to the *sensus communis* of
informed participant debate. But this is not to say, with the
pragmatists or liberal-communitarians, that the only criteria for
judging issues of truth and falsehood (or right and wrong) are those
supplied by some existing community of belief. Rather it is to hold,
like Kant and Habermas, that thinking may always claim the right to
criticize such values just so long as it engages in a *reasoned and
principled* enquiry that respects the conditions for good-faith
utterance in the public sphere of dialogical exchange. Thus, according to O'Neill,

> the reason why Kant is drawn to explicate the authority of reason in
> political metaphors is surely that he sees the problems of cognitive and
> political order as arising in one and the same context. In either case we
> have a plurality of agents or voices (perhaps potential agents or voices)
> and no transcendent or preestablished authority. Reason and justice
> are two aspects to the solution of the problems that arise when an
> uncoordinated plurality of agents is to share a possible world. Hence
> political imagery can illuminate the nature of cognitive order and
> disorientation, just as the vocabulary of reason can be used to charac-

terize social and political order and disorientation. Kant frequently characterizes scepticism as a failure of discursive order, hence as anarchy, just as he characterizes dogmatism (rationalism) as a form of despotism, a triumph of unjust discursive order.[55]

This passage strikes me as an admirably clear-headed statement of the issues confronting present-day thought in the critical and interpretative disciplines. On the one hand there are those (neo-pragmatists, postmodernists, adepts of the 'linguistic turn') who exemplify what O'Neill has to say concerning the 'failure of discursive order', the collapse of truth and reason into so many language-games or cultural 'forms of life'. On the other – though not so much in evidence at present – are the adherents of a monolithic 'Enlightenment' creed which (supposedly) lays claim to an order of transcendent, self-validating truth, and which brooks no opposition from dissenting voices who would challenge its authority to legislate for the conduct of rational debate. But of course it was precisely against such claims – dogmatic impositions of whatever kind, religious or secular – that Kant set out to vindicate the authority of reason as an intersubjective tribunal (or *sensus communis*) wherein they would no longer be able to exert a coercive or distorting pressure.[56]

Hence the close parallel that O'Neill perceives between Kant's treatment of epistemological and socio-political issues. Rationalism becomes 'a form of despotism', a 'triumph of unjust discursive order' in so far as it retreats to the pre-critical standpoint of a truth self-evident to reason and therefore (like the truth-claims of revealed religion) immune to any kind of effectual counter-argument. But it is equally the case – as with postmodernists like Rorty and Lyotard – that the wholesale revolt against Enlightenment thinking gives rise to a form of discursive 'anarchy', a species of cognitive and ethico-political relativism pushed to the point where criticism is powerless against those same (nowadays resurgent) dogmatic truth-claims. Such, after all, is the lesson often derived from Wittgenstein, Lyotard, and other proponents of the view that every language-game (or discourse) disposes of its own *sui generis* criteria, so that the best we can do – in the interests of justice – is acknowledge this open multiplicity of life-forms and give up the attempt to criticize 'truths' or values different from our own. And this (be it noted) at a time when fundamentalist creeds of various description – Christian, Islamic, nationalist, free-market capitalist, and so forth – are vigorously asserting their claim to supersede not only the secular discourse of Enlightenment but also its associated values of participant democracy, liberty of conscience, social welfare, and egalitarian reform. Even a relatively upbeat commentator like Akbar Ahmed in his book *Islam and Postmodernism* is obliged to admit a few caveats with regard to this curious alliance (or working truce) between the high priests and commissars of a new fundamentalism and the postmodern ethos that denies all resort to criticism of dogmatic, irrational, or oppressive systems of belief.[57] For there comes a point – difficult though it may be to determine – at which the good principle of tolerant regard for other people's opinions can lean over into a downright failure of moral and intellectual nerve.

Thus it is all very well for 'advanced' Western theorists to allow themselves this luxury of (in Lyotard's oxymoronic phrase) 'judging without criteria', or treating every case – every language-game or form of life – as equally requiring the principled suspension of our own judgmental norms. But it is a message unlikely to carry much weight with the victims of 'ethnic cleansing' in erstwhile Yugloslavia, with women in the Islamic countries who stand to lose all their hard-won gains if the 'radical' clergy and the hard-line ideologues win out, or with those in the Western 'liberal democracies' who are witnessing the large-scale rollback of rights (often re-named 'benefits') which formed, until recently, the common ground of a broad-based political consensus. At any rate they cannot derive much comfort from an outlook – whatever its impeccably pluralist credentials – that refuses to judge in such matters, treating them rather as so many instances of the narrative–pragmatic 'differend' that always opens up between rival (heterogeneous) ideas of truth and justice. On this account it is wrong – just a piece of Western ethnocentric arrogance – to regard as in any way regressive or undesirable the turn toward cultural 'forms of life' incompatible with our own locally prevailing mores. And the same would apply, presumably, to any internal critic or dissident member of the home community who remarked how wide was the gulf between the rhetoric of liberal democracy and the policies currently pursued in its name. For their argument could only be construed as ignoring the variety of value-laden discourses within that broadly defined cultural sphere, and thus (once again) seeking to suppress the discursive or narrative differend. Indeed it is hard to see how any limit could be drawn to this principle of treating each and every language-game (along with its associated life-form) as intelligible solely on the terms laid down by its own immanent criteria. In which case even the most (to us) objectionable of sexist or socially retrograde practices would be wholly exempt from criticism just so long as they were shown to make sense – or to claim some degree of consensual warrant – within this or that interpretive community.

Such is the upshot of Wittgensteinian thinking as interpreted by commentators like Peter Winch.[58] It is also implicit in Lyotard's claim that only by maximizing narrative differentials – or the range of 'first-order natural narrative pragmatics' – can we possibly respect the singularity of cases and avoid the 'totalitarian' drive to bring them under a common rule. From which it follows, in O'Neill's words, that 'each [particular case] is *sui generis* and in itself a complete example of moral thinking that can provide no basis for prescribing for others, and so, more generally, that moral theories are redundant, since no task remains to be done once examples have been fully articulated'.[59] That is to say, any judgment that exceeds this limit – that presumes to criticize the social values or the cultural life-form manifest in the case under scrutiny – will thereby be claiming a superior vantage-point and (in Lyotard's parlance) committing an infraction of the ethico-discursive differend. It is the same pluralist outlook (often adopted, one should add, with the best moral and political intentions) which enjoins us to respect the diversity of beliefs within and across cultures, and not to use terms like 'fundamentalist', 'reactionary', 'illiberal' and the like as if they possessed a validity transcending such localized differences of view. But what shall we then say of practices – like slavery, clitoridectomy, or widow-burning – that no doubt make sense by the lights of some past or present cultural life-form, but which must surely give pause to anyone who takes this liberal–pluralist line? Or again: what arguments could we muster against those who are currently engaged in genocidal campaigns (or large-scale programmes of 'ethnic cleansing') which undeniably enjoy wide support among members of their own language-group or cultural community? It seems hardly enough to deplore such practices and then enter the standard pluralist caveat: 'but, of course, that is just how we happen to view things, given our local habits of belief'.

Mary Midgley makes this point with admirable clarity in her

essay 'On Trying Out One's New Sword'.[60] Her example is the belief, among Samurai warriors, that the only means to make adequate trial of a freshly-honed blade was to use it in beheading the first stranger encountered along one's way. (An enemy, a relative, friend or acquaintance wouldn't do for this purpose since then one's action might always be tainted by extraneous private motives.) Now of course it may be said – on the relativist view – that we right-thinking modern liberal types are in no strong position to pass judgment on a custom that *we* find utterly barbarous according to our own criteria of civilized conduct. And the same would apply, nearer home, to those bygone practices in European history – public torture, trial by ordeal, witch-burning, and so forth – which we are prone to regard as woeful relics of a pre-enlightenment age. Nowadays anyone who takes this view (or who entertains the notion of 'progress' in whatever regard) is likely to be treated with high contempt as a dupe of that old-style Whiggish 'meta-narrative' which presumed to compare different cultures in point of their advance toward universal standards of humanity and reason. And there is no shortage of commentators (Wittgensteinians, Foucauldians, neo-pragmatists of various political colour) who are ready to press the moral home by instancing the sheer variety of life-forms that arise to confute any such facile progressivist creed. For if ethical values are inextricably tied to their conditions of emergence in this or that culture, then clearly there are no common grounds – no culture-transcendent criteria – by which to judge the issue in any given case. The Samurai could carry on sharpening their bright swords in the knowledge that these would never be rusted by the creeping dew of secular-enlightenment values. Or rather, that any challenge to the sanctity of custom would issue from a standpoint external to the culture in question, and would therefore be *de facto* unable to interpret (let alone criticize or condemn) that culture's distinctive beliefs and practices. Such is the inevitable outcome if one follows the Wittgenstein–Winch line of reasoning that makes all judgments of meaning and value internal to a specific language-game or way of life.

According to O'Neill, it is the chief virtue of Kantian ethics that it resists such forms of localized (consensus-based or communitarian) appeal while also avoiding the opposite ('foundationalist') error that would locate moral judgment in a realm quite apart from the public sphere of informed participant exchange. Kant's approach is notable, she writes, 'for (its) articulation of the relationships between moral theory or principles, illustrative examples and the judgment that is involved in actual moral decisions, none of which he thinks a dispensable part of the moral life'.[62] Nor can such thinking be charged with 'ethnocentrism' if this means the arrogant imposition of quasi-universal (but in fact merely local and contingent) beliefs on the otherwise open multiplicity of cultural life-forms. For it is precisely O'Neill's point – one that finds support from Putnam and Davidson – that we cannot make a start in understanding such differences of view except by assuming certain shared ontological, cognitive, and evaluative commitments. 'Traditional ethnocentrism', the kind that relativists standardly (and rightly) condemn, 'was prepared to override the practices of those beyond its pale; it preached and practised a colonialist ethic, offering to 'natives' at most the opportunity for "them" to assimilate to "us".' But the problem reappears, as we have seen, in those liberal-sounding versions of the communitarian ethic which acknowledge the relativity (or the culture-specific character) of their own as well as of other belief-systems. Such mild ethnocentrism, in O'Neill's words,

> has nothing to say to those who live beyond 'our' local pale; in the face of a world in which adherents of distinct practices meet increasingly it proposes a retreat to the cosiness of 'our' shared world and tradition. Perhaps it is not surprising that such a conception of ethics should flourish mainly in the academies of a former imperial power, and that it should focus primarily on judging what has been done. Precisely because of the transience of ethical practices, to which Wittgensteinian writers draw our attention, we cannot easily lead our lives without asking questions which are not just internal to but about local practices.[64]

In short, the communitarian doctrine is apt to rebound upon anyone who adopts it – even with the best motives – as a hedge against ethnocentric prejudice. For on this view there is simply no way that we could get to appreciate the *reasons* (as opposed to the predisposed cultural habits of mind) that lead other people to think and judge as they do.[65] That is to say, we should always be placed – like Quine's 'radical translator' – in the position of a good-willed but sceptical observer with nothing to go on save his or her own (strictly local and contingent) beliefs. In which case, moreover, those beliefs would provide the only possible criteria by which to evaluate such instances of cultural difference. So it is that the liberal–pluralist ethos – along with its communitarian, Wittgensteinian, and postmodern–

pragmatist offshoots – starts out from an attitude of decent respect for the diversity of cultural life-forms, but ends up by tacitly endorsing a kind of *faute de mieux* ethnocentric outlook.

My point in all this is that ontological scepticism – of the sort now pretty much obligatory among 'advanced' cultural theorists – necessarily gives rise to such disabling consequences in the ethico-political sphere. For, as O'Neill remarks, '(w)hat we need, minimally, if there is to be some possibility of a more than locally comprehensible applied ethics, are some ways of appraising and judging the sorts of cases with which we have to deal'.[66] And this in turn requires – contrary to the current *doxa* – that judgment should be exercised (and truth-claims assessed) *not* just according to some local set of language-specific or culture-based criteria but in light of the best available knowledge and the best, most humanly-accountable values. Such is the *sensus communis* as Kant conceived it: the jointly epistemological and evaluative quest for principles of reason that would point beyond the limiting horizon of present, *de facto* communal belief. Thus:

> [w]hereas 'common sense' is used to refer to understandings that are actually shared, in an actual community or more widely, the *sensus communis* consists of (those) principles or maxims that constrain understandings, indeed practices of communication, that can be shared in any *possible* community ... They articulate the self-discipline of thinking that will be required if there is to be communication among a plurality whose members are not antecedently coordinated.[67]

This last point is crucial since it marks the distinction between an ethics grounded in the prior authority of this or that (possibly coercive) communal code and one that acknowledges only those 'constraints' – rather, those enabling conditions – that answer to a shared human interest in the project of emancipatory critique. To this extent O'Neill is fully in agreement with Habermas, although (oddly enough) his name figures nowhere in her book. What unites these thinkers – and sets them both at odds with the current relativist drift – is their defence of that continuing critical impulse within the philosophic discourse of modernity that doesn't fall prey to the routine charge of so-called 'foundationalist' thinking. For this charge can appear plausible only on a Rorty-style reading of intellectual history that confuses Kant with Descartes, or the *sensus communis* of participant debate with the self-grounding certitude of the sovereign Cartesian *cogito*.

Hence the massively distorted image of 'Enlightenment' reason put around by postmodernists, neo-pragmatists, and others, often (one suspects) on the basis of a slender acquaintance with the relevant texts and contexts. Nor does it require any great investment of scholarly labour to perceive how utterly wide of the mark is this bugbear characterization. One only need compare (say) Lyotard's prejudicial talk of enlightened 'meta-narratives', 'master-discourses', monopolistic capitalized Truth, and so forth with the account offered by a well-informed intellectual historian like Peter Gay.[68] What then becomes clear – no doubt to the suprise of readers bred up on the doxastic postmodern view – is the sheer absurdity of equating 'Enlightenment' either with one historically delimited period of recent European thought or with a fixed set of doctrines laying claim to some ultimate (quasi-theological) truth. Even the most cursory reading of Gay's two volumes is sufficient to dispel the latter misconception. Never has there been a more fissile, internally fractured, and disputacious movement of thought than the enterprise launched by the French *philosophes* and raised to a higher point of critical reflection by Kant and subsequent thinkers. In fact this was not just a period trait but a defining characteristic of the Enlightenment project, committed as it was – and as Kant most explicitly proclaimed – to a principle of freedom in the questioning of received ideas and values. But such an attitude cannot be maintained without presupposing certain shared criteria as to what shall count as an adequately argued, a good-faith, or ethically accountable submission. It is the same point that is made (in somewhat minimalist fashion) by Putnam and Davidson, or again – with wider argumentative scope – by O'Neill and Habermas.

To bring such a varied assortment of thinkers under the 'Enlightenment' rubric might seem a merely honorific deployment of the term, or at any rate one that stretches its meaning far beyond the limits of responsible usage. But it is – I would argue – an extension warranted both strategically (as a counter to widespread pejorative inflections of the word) and also, in principle, by way of denoting what links some otherwise disparate movements of thought. 'Enlightenment' in this sense is a name for that distinctive, historically emergent (but by no means period-specific) set of ideas and values which may be characterized – very briefly – as the active antithesis of everything represented by the current postmodernist turn. Most important is the threefold claim: that human beings are able to communicate across differences of language, culture, and belief; that such communication is possible on account of their shared knowledge-constitutive interests; and moreover, that those interests have an ethical as well as a cognitive (or epistemological) bearing, since the project of emancipatory critique is closely bound up with the capacity for distinguishing true from false – distorted or ideological – habits of belief. Postmodernism may be characterized, conversely, as a point-for-point denial of all three claims, along with an ethic (or a politics) of cultural 'difference' which views Enlightenment as a discourse of unitary Truth, bent upon effacing or suppressing such heterogeneity. Whence Lyotard's triple injunction: that we should 'wage a war on totality, . . . be witnesses to the unpresentable, . . . activate the differences and save the honour of the name'.[69] For it is only by maintaining this ultra-nominalist stance – this refusal to generalize beyond the level of 'first-order natural' speech-act pragmatics – that thought can avoid the manifest injustice which comes of discounting the narrative differend.

Of course (as I have said) there is nothing to complain about here if the position comes down to a decent respect for the variety of human values, beliefs, and satisfactions. After all, such an outlook is not only compatible with Enlightenment thinking but constitutes its strongest claim on our allegiance as critical intellectuals whose freedom to question the currency of orthodox belief is one that we inherit very largely from that same tradition of dissident thought. This would make 'enlightenment' a term more or less synonymous with the critique of unwarranted doctrinal impositions – especially the truth-claims of revealed religion – carried on by thinkers from Erasmus to Montaigne, Spinoza, Kant, and their latter-day demythologizing heirs. Indeed – as will be evident to those with a knowledge of the relevant background history – it is this tradition that is tacitly invoked by critics and theorists who eagerly proclaim the eclipse of 'grand narratives', the demise of the 'transcendental signified', the obsolescence of any absolute, unitary Truth, and so forth. In this sense one could argue that just about every school of present-day critical thought, from deconstruction to New Historicism, acknowledges its debt – whether wittingly or not – to the legacy of Enlightenment critique. It is a project carried on in the deconstructive questioning of 'logocentric' values and truth-claims, in the effort to redeem those marginalized voices that have suffered the violence of colonial rule or the enormous condescension of posterity, and also – despite his anti-enlightenment rhetoric – in Foucault's genealogies of power/knowledge.[70]

That is to say, these thinkers take for granted a whole range of crucial distinctions – as between truth and falsehood, reason and rhetoric, real human interests and their distorted (ideological) representation – which no amount of *de rigueur* postmodern scepticism can entirely conceal from view. Such projects would lack any meaning or purpose (would indeed be quite unintelligible) were it not for their tacitly acknowledged commitment to those same principles and values. Historically they stand in a line of descent from the critique of revelation – of truth-claims vested in a single self-authorizing discourse – which ousted theology from its sovereign role as arbiter in issues of intellectual conscience, and which thus secured an expanding sphere of freedom in the natural and human sciences. Moreover, it is this history of hard-won progress in the right to think and criticize that postmodernists would blithely revoke when they denounce 'enlightenment' as a thing of the past, an authoritarian discourse aimed towards suppressing all signs of cultural difference or alterity. For the very terms in which their arguments are couched – historical, sociological, ethico-political – are terms that quite literally *make no sense* if removed from the validating context of enlightened thought.

This is what Habermas means when he writes of the 'performative contradiction' involved in all such wholesale sceptical assaults on the philosophic discourse of modernity. It is particularly evident in Foucault's case, since here one finds all the resources of classical scholarship and criticism – not to mention those of philosophic argument and textual exegesis – deployed with a view to discrediting the values of reason and truth, or revealing their complicity with the will-to-power over minds and bodies alike. Derrida makes the same point about Foucault – to subtler and more telling effect – when he shows how impossible is the latter's claim (in his book *Madness and Civilization*) to be speaking the very language of madness as against the tyrannizing discourse of post-Cartesian reason. What Foucault fails to recognise is the flat contradiction involved in presenting an elaborately argued and documented case against the very same standards (of rational, scholarly, and critical argumentation) which his book avowedly disowns. On the one hand – doubtless for strategic purposes – Foucault narrows his genealogical sights to equate 'reason' with just that singular episode (the Cartesian *cogito*) and just that arguably consequent history (the 'great confinement') which together allow him to press the case for condemning rationality and all its works. Thus '(t)o all appearances it is reason that he [Foucault] interns, but, like Descartes, he chooses the reason of yesterday as his target and not the possibility of meaning in general'.[71] For on the other hand – by the strictest order of discursive necessity – Foucault is constrained to abide by the ground-rules of reasoned critical argument even in the act of denouncing them with all the rhetorical means at his disposal.

Thus in Derrida's words:

> if discourse and philosophical communication (that is, language itself) are to have an intelligible meaning, that is to say, if they are to conform to their essence and vocation as discourse, they must simultaneously in fact and in principle escape madness. They must carry normality within themselves ... By its essence, the sentence is normal ... whatever the health or madness of him who propounds it, or whom it passes through, on whom, in whom it is articulated. In its most impoverished syntax, logos is reason and, indeed, a historical reason.[72]

This is a version of the transcendental argument – or the mode of reasoning *a priori* from the 'conditions of possibility' for thought and language in general – which philosophers since Plato have often used and which takes its most developed, systematic form in the writings of Kant. What is distinctive about Derrida's use of it – a point brought out with admirable clarity by Rodolphe Gasché – is the fact that he typically fastens on the conditions of *im*possibility that prevent certain thinkers (among them Plato, Rousseau, Kant, Husserl, and Saussure) from maintaining a consistent position with regard to issues in the philosophy of mind, knowledge, and language.[73] This is precisely his point about Foucault: that the latter falls into manifest absurdity when he claims that *Madness and Civilization* is not only a book *about* the history of 'madness' but one that is written *in the very language and from the deepest interior of* the discourse of insanity itself. Foucault could not have advanced a single proposition on the subject – let alone an entire work of sophisticated argument and erudite scholarship – without undermining his own professed objective at every turn. Quite simply, reason is not an option in the sense that one could leave it behind (or opt out of it) for the sake of promoting some radically 'other' kind of discourse, some language on the far side of truth, normativity, 'logocentric' thinking, or whatever.

That Foucault imagines such a break to be possible is a sign of his labouring under a twofold confusion. One is the idea that Descartes can be taken as having somehow inaugurated the 'age of reason' and, along with it, those various forms of repressive institutional regime – from the asylum to psychiatric medicine – which (so it is argued) represent the dark side of enlightened thought. But this is to mistake the peculiar character of Descartes' 'hyperbolical' thought-experiment for an instance of what Derrida calls 'reason in general'. That is to say, it ignores the *inescapable* requirement that a work like Foucault's – a discourse on or of madness – should itself make sense according to criteria of logic, rational argument, critique of historical source-texts, etc. And the second confusion, following from this, is his treatment of 'reason' as a monolithic discourse, always on the side of instituted power and repressive (instrumental) rationality. For it is because he holds such a reductive, quasi-Hobbesian conception of 'power/knowledge' that Foucault is thus driven to discount all appeals to reason in its other (i.e. critical-emancipatory) role.

Hence, as several commentators have noted, the curious conjunction in Foucault's work of a passionate address to issues of social injustice with a flat refusal to provide that work with any normative basis for judgments of truth and falsehood (or right and wrong) beyond the idea of localized strategic intervention.[74] All that is left, as in *Madness and Civilization*, is an ill-defined notion of absolute alterity – of the excluded or marginalized 'other' – whose locus shifts successively from text to text as Foucault engages the various 'discourses' of psychiatry, criminology, penal institutions, confessional practices, gender-role enforcement, and so forth. In each case this 'other' is conceived in purely oppositional terms, that is, as a subject (or anonymous collectivity of interests) whose claims can be honoured only by acknowledging the sheer gulf that exists between their 'discourse' and ours, or the language of madness, criminal deviance, sexual alterity etc. and the 'enlightened' discourse that would falsely presume to articulate their difference in a language acceptable to us present-day (liberal–reformist) types. What this amounts to, in effect, is a transposition of Saussurean linguistic theory – language as a network of relations and differences 'without positive terms' – into the sphere of social and ethico-political thought.[75] On this point Foucault is wholly in agreement with Lyotard. We commit an infraction of the speech-act or narrative 'differend' when we seek to bring conflicting interests under a common rule, or to legislate for others on principles deriving from our own (no matter how 'progressive' or 'enlightened') habits of thought. The only means of respecting their absolute otherness – their entitlement to a discourse radically incommensurable with our own – is to suspend all judgments of right and wrong save those that promote the rightful multiplicity of language-games and which thus equate wrong with any move to restrict or suppress this open plurality.

IV

Textuality, difference, and cultural otherness

One will not have far to seek for such talk of the 'other' as a touchstone of postmodern ethics, politics, and gender issues. Alterity is raised to a kind of shibboleth, a guard against those 'totalitarian' or 'homogenizing' habits of thought which seek to reduce cultural difference to the dead level of a master-discourse premised on the truth of its own universalist concepts and categories. This discourse is variously identified with male ('phallogocentric') values, with the privileging of concept over metaphor in philosophic thought, with the demotion of ethics *vis-à-vis* epistemology (which, according to Emmanuel Levinas, has been the hallmark of philosophy from its Greek origins to the present), and – above all – with the Western Enlightenment meta-narrative of reason, progress and truth.[76] Other versions of this argument include the idea of dialectics in whatever form (especially Hegelian or Marxist) as a discourse aimed towards truth at the end of enquiry, and hence – once again – as a technique for suppressing any differences of view along the way.[77] It is against such manifestations of the discursive will-to-power (equated *tout court*, in Nietzschean style, with the philosophic 'will-to-truth') that theorists have come up with a range of strategies for disrupting its self-assured sovereign claims. What they all involve is some notion of the 'other' – of a radical difference beyond the utmost of philosophy's recuperative powers – which can somehow be shown to perform that work of disruption.[78] Hence the almost ritual invocations of alterity – sexual difference, cultural difference, 'heterogeneous' language-games, epistemological breaks, narrative differends etc. – whose mere recital is often taken as sufficient guarantee that we have at last come out from under that bad old discourse of oppressive monological reason.

What tends to get ignored in all this self-congratulatory post-modern talk is the fact that such 'otherness' is the merest of rhetorical place-fillers. More precisely: it is a pseudo-concept or a kind of all-purpose alibi for the consciences of those on the 'cultural' (often the ex-Marxist) left who have lost all sense of moral and political purpose, and have sought to rationalize this predicament by declaring an end to those values bound up with the project of emancipatory critique. One can see this most clearly in Lyotard's case, where the rhetoric of 'heterogeneous' language-games goes along with a species of out-and-out ethical intuitionism which renders 'justice' a matter of deciding in favour of this or that plaintiff with reference solely to the voice of the 'other' within us, no matter what the facts or the ethical rights and wrongs as they appear to our normal (waking or rational) powers of reflective judgment.[79] Here as so often, the 'other' is brought in – by analogy with the Kantian sublime – as that which confronts thinking at the limit where cognitive and evaluative phrase-regimes are forced to acknowledge the absolute lack of common measure between them. And it is here also, according to Lyotard, that we come to recognize the strictly non-negotiable issue between rival litigants in any given case. For we commit an injustice – a suppression of the differend – if we think to adjudicate their dispute by presuming that they share at least some measure of common ground as regards the relevance of (e.g.) factual, ethical, or socio-political criteria. On the contrary: what is required of us is an *absolute and principled* suspension of judgment, to the point where nothing remains of that inveterate drive to assimilate (or homogenize) the voice of the other.

In one or another version this idea is so widespread among present-day cultural theorists that I hardly need enumerate instances to make my case. It is most prominent in fields like anthropology, ethnography, and comparative literature, disciplines that have naturally been quick to register the shift from a colonial to a post-colonial order of relationship in their passage across and between cultures. It is not surprising that these geo-political changes should have induced some likewise far-reaching shifts in the discourse of the human sciences. Among them may be counted that preoccupation with themes of cultural 'otherness' which has becomne such a characteristic feature of present-day critical thought. The most useful cover-term for these tendencies is probably the phrase 'thick description', coined by Clifford Geertz to denominate the kind of ethnographic writing that strives to give a vivid and detailed impression of (to us) alien life-forms, while eschewing the temptation to interpret or judge them according to our own cultural norms.[80] Along with this goes a recommendation that we should loosen up those old disciplinary constraints that once served as markers of professional expertise, but which now constitute a hindrance to creative scholarship. Thus for Geertz – as for others like Rorty – there is no longer any point in seeking to distinguish between (say) 'descriptive' and 'theoretical' texts, first-hand narratives and analytic commentary, or what ethnographers do when writing up their fieldwork and what they offer by way of 'higher-level' (methodological) reflection. Such distinctions are at best a matter of convenience, a pragmatic adjustment to publishing conventions or the current academic division of labour. At worst they perform a policing function, a bar to the kinds of open-textured, exploratory writing that Geertz endeavours to promote. Moreover, they are complicit with that ethnocentric bias – the bane of old-style anthropological research – which treats other life-forms (or 'primitive' cultures) as fit material for the scholar's more enlightened interpretive techniques.

Hence no doubt the great appeal of Geertz's work for those (the New Historicists among them) who are similarly keen to 'deconstruct' what they see as a range of pernicious hierarchical distinctions. Of these, the most offensive – since most closely bound up with the discourse of cultural imperialism – are the distinctions commonly held to obtain on the one hand between 'literary' and 'nonliterary' texts (the latter including various kinds of background or ancillary source material), and on the other between works in the 'high' (canonical) tradition and works of a lesser – perhaps subliterary – status. I have no wish here to engage in the controversy between upholders and bashers of the canon.[81] More to the point, for present purposes, is the question what results from this levelling move not so much with regard to issues of literary value but as concerns those various orders of discourse – poetic, narrative, theoretical, social-documentary, and so forth – which the New Historicists would treat as belonging to a field of endless intertextual crossings and exchanges. Their aim in all this is to knock away the various disciplinary and cultural props which have served to uphold what can now be seen as a narrowly ethnocentric order of values and priorities. It is also – as with Geertz – an approach that claims to democratize the intercourse of cultures past and present by effacing those markers of superior epistemic status that attach to the language of authorized (mostly first-world) theorists and commentators *vis-à-vis* the various materials they are given to interpret. For if everything is regarded as a 'kind of writing' – ethnographic samples, fieldwork reports, narrative case-histories, methodological reflections, etc. – then there can be no question of any one such discourse setting up as the privileged voice of reason and truth. Two main benefits are held to follow from this. The ethnographer or critic is thereby freed to practise a more adventurous, exploratory style of writing, one that no longer pays homage to the false ideals of detached ('meta-linguistic') objectivity and rigour. But also, more importantly, such writing gives voice to those other (hitherto repressed or marginalized) cultures, communities, and beliefs which would else get a hearing only on condition that their witness be subject to a higher-level order of interpretive enquiry.[82]

In short, there are some large claims vested in this turn towards a broadly hermeneutic (more precisely: a postmodern–narrative–textualist) paradigm for the human sciences. In Derridean parlance it is presented as the move from a 'restricted economy' of value-laden binary distinctions (text/context, language/meta-language, metaphor/concept, and the like) to a 'general economy' where texts circulate – and cultures coexist – in the absence of any such putative master-discourse.[83] It is the same utopian gesture – 'utopian' in the strictest sense of that term – which characterizes all versions of the textualist argument, that is to say, the idea that experience and reality are constructed in and through language, so that changes in the writing (the textual inscription) of 'otherness' or cultural difference are bound to bring about some fundamental shift in the order of power-relations. But there are, as I have said, serious problems with this argument when one attempts to think its implications through whether as a question in the philosophy of the human sciences or as a matter of practical everyday ethics. Among them is the point raised in various ways by Davidson, Putnam, and O'Neill: that relativist talk of 'otherness' (or radical 'heterogeneity') can easily become – as it does with Rorty – just a catch-all pretext for retreating into our own kind of cosy parochial wisdom.

This case can be put very simply. What it takes to give others the credit for holding views different from (and maybe better than) our own is the basic supposition that they, like us, have an interest in getting things right, in criticizing false or irrational beliefs, and in dispelling the kinds of illusion (as well as injustice) that arise from ignorance, prejudice, or unequal access to the relevant information-sources. This in turn requires a more substantive conception of knowledge and human interests than anything provided by the post-modern–textualist paradigm. For on the latter view – promoted by literary adepts like Barthes and by Foucault in his early texts – the subject becomes just an effect of language, a figment of the short-lived humanist imaginary, one whose claims to truth and self-knowledge will soon show up as the merest of transcendental illusions.[84] At this point, so Foucault prophesies, 'man' will disappear like a figure drawn in sand at the ocean's edge, his lineaments erased by the incoming tide. Having once emerged briefly as a specular image in the interstices of language (or 'discourse'), the subject will dissolve back into its element and cease the vain quest – the chimerical Kantian endeavour – to define its own knowledge-constitutive interests, its moral autonomy or powers of reflective judgment. Of course it will be said that this is all old hat, and that Foucault moved on in his later writings to reopen the questions of truth, knowledge, and ethical agency. But he did so – as I have argued elsewhere – only by way of an aestheticized discourse of autonomous self-creation which still treats the subject as a figment of language, albeit a language that is somehow chosen (like one of Rorty's elective 'final vocabularies') from the range currently on offer.[85] So far from resolving or displacing the Kantian antinomy of free will and determinism Foucault gives it the additional (linguistic) turn which forces subjectivity into an endless spiral of utterly determinate 'subject-positions' and strictly unthinkable notions of absolute freedom.

New Historicism inherits this dead-end predicament without the least sign of acknowledging its problematic character. That is to say, it follows Foucault in reducing all questions of knowledge, judgment and ethics to the level of an intra-discursive force-field, an agonistic play of resistances or power/knowledge effects where the subject is just a ghost in the linguistic machine, an epiphenomenon of discourse. Nor is it in any way fortuitous that in drawing out the aporias of Foucault's position one is led to invoke these Cartesian metaphors and echoes of Gilbert Ryle on Descartes.[86] For there is a similar problem with Foucault: how to overcome the deep-laid conflict that exists between a thoroughgoing determinism as applied to the body and its various disciplinary-discursive regimes, and the necessary margin of free-will required to envisage any ethics or politics worth the name. Small wonder that much of the current debate around Foucault, New Historicism, and other such schools of 'advanced' critical thought reads like an unwitting re-run of arguments in the wake of Cartesian dualism. What links them is a drastic dichotomy between, on the one hand, the subject (in Lacanian terms, the 'subject-presumed-to-know') conceived in ideal illusory abstraction from the physical or bodily domain, and on the other a realm of implacably determinist forces and drives which renders such illusions untenable. The great difference between them, of course, is that Descartes strives unavailingly to keep that illusion in place, while Foucault seizes every opportunity to belabour the Cartesian *cogito*, the Kantian 'transcendental subject' and their manifold socio-historical effects.[87]

Such, as we have seen, is his argument in *Madness and Civilization* with regard to the complicity of Cartesian reason in episodes like the 'great confinement' and other examples of man's inhumanity to man. But his case appears much less convincing if one asks, with Habermas, what *reasons* Foucault can offer – factual, ethical, or principled reasons – for bringing that history to book (so to speak) as an instance of certain determinate abuses in the discourse of oppressive instrumental rationality. For he is working with so impoverished a notion of 'reason' – and so minimal a conception of the subject – that there seems no alternative to the power/knowledge nexus that defines every aspect of human social interaction. In short, Foucault deprives himself of any normative (i.e., reasoned and principled) grounds on which to mount his otherwise passionate case as regards the great legacy of suffering, injustice, and human waste brought about by such specific perversions of the rationalist project.[88] In Habermasian terms he fails to distinguish between the various spheres of reason – instrumental (problem-solving), ethicopolitical, aesthetic or 'world-disclosive', etc. – and hence fails to see how encroachments by the first on to the others' domain may result in just the kinds of large-scale abuse that his texts so persistently denounce.[89] By reducing 'reason' to its lowest common denominator (instrumental rationality) Foucault in effect closes off any prospect of progressive or emancipatory change. And by the same token he consigns the subject – the bare forked creature of Cartesian rationalism – to a ghostly existence on the fringes of a 'discourse' (or a textual multiplicity of discourses-in-conflict) which likewise leaves no escape route open from the prison-house of language.

It is a similar point that Derrida makes (in 'Cogito and the History of Madness') when he remarks on the strict impossibility of Foucault's exorbitant claim, that is, his desire to assume the very voice of the 'other', to write not merely a book *about* madness but one that inhabits its very language, authentically re-lives its experience, and thus brings to light a whole buried history which constitutes the shadow-side of enlightenment thought. As Derrida reads it there is less difference between Descartes' and Foucault's projects than the latter would wish to believe. If Descartes conducts his 'hyperbolic' thought-experiment with the object of finally regaining epistemic, ontological, and religious security, Foucault re-stages the Cartesian episode with a view to undermining those same delusory certitudes. But in the end – and by the strictest order of logical necessity – Foucault can treat of that notional 'other' only in a language that interprets the discourse of madness in humanly intelligible terms. Thus:

> Any philosopher or speaking subject (and the philosopher is but the speaking subject par excellence) who must invoke madness from the *interior* of thought (and not only from within the body or some other extrinsic agency), can do so only in the realm of the *possible* and in the language of fiction or the fiction of language. Thereby, through his own language, he reassures himself against any actual madness – which must sometimes appear quite talkative, another problem – and can keep his distance, the distance indispensable for continuing to speak and to live. But this is not a weakness or a search for security proper to a given historical language (for example, the search for security in the Cartesian style), but is rather inherent in the essence and very project of all language in general; and even in the language of those who are apparently the maddest; and even and above all in the language of those who, by their praise of madness, by their complicity with it, measure themselves against the greatest possible proximity to madness.[90]

This is not to say – far from it – that Foucault's is a wholly misconceived project or an enterprise marked at every point by signs of intellectual bad faith. On the contrary: Derrida goes out of his way to acknowledge the necessity of raising these questions, the probity of Foucault's scholarship, and the justice (as well as the animating passion) which characterize that work at its best. His response to Derrida – published in the second edition of *Folie et déraison* – is evidence enough that Foucault failed to grasp the proffered olive-branch.[91] Deconstruction is here reviled as a 'determined little pedagogy', a masterly technique for drilling students into the doctrine that nothing exists outside the text, and hence that they had much better stick to the seminar-room rather than involve themselves with issues of real-world social and political concern.

In this polemical context one should not perhaps make too much of Foucault's thus recycling the familiar charge – the idea of deconstruction as a textualist variant on a transcendental–solipsist theme – which has long been the standard reproach among commentators lacking any first-hand acquaintance with Derrida's work. More revealing in this case is the fact that the charge can be turned back against Foucault, despite his very overt engagement with questions that he accuses Derrida of ignoring. For it is precisely Derrida's point that one can have no access to the 'other' – to modes of knowledge or experience that exist (so it seems) at the furthest remove from our own – except by way of a language that presupposes at least some measure of shared conceptual ground. It is in this sense that Derrida can claim (no doubt thus adding to Foucault's exasperation) that 'the philosopher is but the speaking subject par excellence'.[92] What he means by this cryptic sentence can I think be spelled out as follows. 'Philosophy' is not – as Foucault would have it in his short way of dealing with Descartes – *purely and simply* a form of self-aggrandizing discourse that deploys concepts like truth, reason, and the 'transcendental subject' in order to promote its own imperious interests and exclude the 'other' from its sovereign domain. To be sure, it has very often been put to such uses, co-opted in the service of a false (ethnocentric or dogmatic) universalism that identifies 'reason' with the truth-claims and values of some particular interest-group empowered to dictate what shall count as reason and truth. Few thinkers have done more than Derrida to expose these structures of deep-laid prejudice – this sublimated 'white mythology' – in the texts of Western philosophy from Plato to Husserl. But he is none the less justified in arguing, *contra* Foucault, that it is not 'philosophy' in general that is thereby compromised but certain kinds of discourse that have captured and exploited the rhetoric of 'truth' and 'reason'. One will hardly understand how this has come about if one opts for a notional counter-rhetoric – a language of 'madness' or the absolute 'other' – beyond all the bounds of rational intelligibility. In so far as s/he speaks always and necessarily 'from the *interior* of thought' – on the face of it a thoroughly 'logocentric' standpoint, and hence (one might think) an odd phrase for Derrida to use – the philosopher is compelled to question any discourse that stakes its radical credentials on the claim to issue from 'within the body or some other extrinsic agency'. For quite simply there is no making sense of such claims when advanced – as they must be – by a subject whose language (whose every sentence or enunciative gesture) belongs to that same order of discourse which they seek to overthrow from outside.

This applies just as much to Foucault's anti-Cartesian discourse on madness as to Descartes' original thought-experiment with its purportedly reassuring upshot. In each case, as Derrida remarks, 'speech, confined to this temporal rhythm of crisis and reawakening, is able to open the space for discourse only by imprisoning madness'.[93] Which is also to say that any address to the 'other' – any attempt to think beyond the categories of 'logocentric' reason – will either take the form of an immanent critique (in which case it cannot break altogether with those categories) or otherwise, *per impossibile*, be couched in a language wholly unintelligible to us or anyone else. Foucault was therefore wrong to dismiss Derrida's essay as a mere exercise in textualist mystification. On the contrary, it raises issues of considerable moment for just the kind of enterprise undertaken by Foucault and the New Historicists after him. In their view the only way forward for cultural criticism in a postmodern, postenlightenment, post-colonial epoch is one that abjures all appeals to reason – or to outmoded concepts like *Ideologiekritik* – whose effect is always to promote some higher-level discourse of truth, some presumptive 'meta-language' (Marxist, structuralist, psychoanalytic, or whatever) which merely reproduces byegone relations of power/knowledge. Hence – to repeat – the rhetoric of radical 'otherness', of absolute difference or heterogeneity whereby (so it is thought) those dominant structures can at last be overturned.

But such arguments are open to precisely the criticism that Derrida brings against Foucault: that the 'other' thus evoked is the merest of nominal entities, one that stands in for the absence of any reasoned and principled engagement with these issues. And a similar objection may be raised to the idea that we best do justice to those marginalized 'others' of Western (ethnocentric or phallocratic) culture by bringing them all under the rubric of a generalized textuality (or economy of difference) that somehow constitutes a challenge to existing forms of hegemonic discourse. For here again one has to ask what 'justice' can amount to if proclaimed on behalf of a notional 'other' whose interests, whose meanings, and whose very life-history are represented (in effect) as constructions out of this or that preferred mode of latterday textual exegesis. In short, we are back with the besetting problem of cultural relativism, namely the fact – as noted by Putnam and O'Neill – that such attitudes very easily flip over into a kind of *faute de mieux* methodological solipsism that is all the more deceptive for maintaining a rhetoric of other-regarding principle.

V

Ethics and alterity: Derrida on Levinas

This issue is at the heart of Derrida's essay 'Violence and Metaphysics', an early text devoted to the work of the philosopher Emmanuel Levinas.[94] It can aptly be characterized as a *critique* of Levinasian ethics, and this in the strictest sense of that term, despite the many well-known cautionary passages where Derrida counsels us not to confuse deconstruction with (for instance) a 'simple progressive critique in the style of the Enlightenment'.[95] For Levinas, the history of Western (post-Hellenic) thought is marked always by the privilege accorded to epistemological questions, and hence by its failure to recognize the absolute primacy of ethical concerns.[96] These latter can be broached only through a thinking that acknowledges the claim of the other, that is to say, of an other whose intransigent ethical demand – whose right to exist in a realm quite apart from our own knowledge-constitutive interests – requires the suspension of all pre-existent concepts and categories. From Plato to Husserl, philosophy has refused this demand by treating ethics (in however serious or respectful a fashion) as that which comes after – and depends upon – some adequate theory of truth, knowledge, or reflective self-understanding. Thus '(b)y making the other . . . the ego's phenomenon, constituted by analogical appresentation on the basis of belonging to the ego's own sphere, Husserl allegedly missed the infinite alterity of the other, reducing it to the same'.[97] Phenomenology figures as merely the latest – and no doubt most resourceful – stage of advance in a tradition that has always sought to avoid this challenge to its powers of recuperative grasp. Only by relinquishing the epistemic will-to-truth (or its desire to treat the other on terms laid down by its own 'egological' categories of thought) can philosophy accede to an ethical wisdom, an openness to 'infinite alterity' that would break with this deep-laid logocentric drive. More simply, in Levinas's words: 'the other, as other, is not only an alter ego. It is what I myself am not.'[98]

One can well understand the recent upsurge of interest in Levinas's work among thinkers of a broadly postmodernist persuasion, some of them – like Simon Critchley – acclaiming it as an ethical extension or fulfilment of Derrida's deconstructive enterprise.[99] There is also an obvious affinity with those notions of cultural difference or 'otherness' that play such a prominent role in the thinking of Foucault and the New Historicists. But Derrida's essay should at least give pause to anyone impressed by these points of resemblance. For it is, to repeat, a *critique* of Levinasian ethics that combines – as usual with Derrida – a minute and faithful attentiveness to the text in hand with a questioning of the very conditions of possibility for a thinking that would claim to come out on the far side of all inherited ('logocentric' or 'metaphysical') categories of thought. 'It is impossible', Derrida writes, 'to encounter the alter ego (in the very form of the encounter described by Levinas), impossible to respect it in experience and in language, if this other, in its alterity, does not *appear* for an ego (in general).'[100] And again: '(o)ne could neither speak, nor have any sense of the totally other, if there was not a phenomenenon of the totally other, or evidence of the totally other as such.'[101] From which it follows that we must have knowledge of the other – understand him or her by analogy with our own experience – if 'otherness' is not to become just a form of inverted autism, an empty locus upon which to project our ideas of a radical (hence wholly abstract and unknowable) difference. Thus for Derrida as also for Habermas, Davidson, and Putnam – despite their otherwise very disparate lines of approach – there is a level of shared understanding prerequisite to any ethics (or any theory of mutual obligation) that would seek to avoid this ultimate impasse. Nor is it the case that the turn towards language (or discourse) as a basis for treating these issues necessarily leads to some version of the postmodern incommensurability-thesis. For it can just as well be taken as yet further evidence that the thesis reduces to manifest nonsense if carried to the point where understanding is dissolved in a rhetoric of 'otherness' devoid of intelligible content.

It is in this very literal sense of the phrase that the other is understood as an 'alter ego', one whose demands are demands *upon us* as subjects with a similar claim to such treatment. Levinas's notion of 'infinite alterity' must remain just that – a notional appeal devoid of ethical substance – unless it acknowledges (what can scarcely be denied) the need to *put oneself in the other's place* in order to recognize that claim. In defending Husserl against Levinas's charge Derrida is also denying the very possibility of an ethics that would somehow forswear any recourse to epistemological categories. That is to say, the alter ego is construed as such – as rightfully enjoying that degree of autonomous selfhood – only on condition that s/he possesses certain knowledge-constitutive interests, along with the freedom to act, will, and judge in accord with those same interests. Of course this relation between knowledge and will – or cognitive understanding and practical reason – remains very much a topic of debate among philosophers in the post-Kantian tradition. Indeed it is the single most vexing issue for anyone who seeks on the one hand to vindicate our freedom (or autonomy) as moral agents while on the other conceding that such freedom is meaningless – 'absurd', as some nihilists would have it – if exercised without a knowledge of the relevant facts, circumstances, or truth-conditions. That Kant was very far from resolving this (perhaps unresolvable) issue is all the same no reason to count postmodernists like Lyotard justified when they equate ethics with an order of radical heterogeneity whose emblem is the Kantian sublime, and whose character is such as to block all appeals to cognitive or epistemic criteria. For here again the 'other' can no longer be construed as an alter ego, a subject in whom this relationship between knowledge, reason, and will is likewise set about with all manner of antinomies or complex mediations. Rather it takes on an alien nature, a resistance or opacity to thought which stands in the way of any possible intersubjective understanding.

In fact – as Derrida notes in his essay on Levinas – there is a risk that such thinking will reproduce the most traditional of philosophic gestures. That is to say, it treats the other (like Foucault's 'madness') as a discourse of absolute alterity which for that very reason – by virtue of its intransigent otherness – becomes more an object of philosophic scrutiny than an instance of subjectively intelligible language. And so it transpires, through this most ironic of reversals, that the attempt to do justice to the other by acknowledging his or her unconditional difference produces what amounts to a gesture of containment, a move whereby that other is envisaged as the mute, non-signifying matter of philosophic discourse. For is it not the case,

Derrida asks, that 'empiricism has always been determined . . . as *nonphilosophy*: as the philosophical pretention to nonphilosophy, the inability to justify oneself, to come to one's own aid as speech?'[102] By the same token, any ethics of 'absolute alterity' – in so far as such an ethics is thinkable at all – has the untoward consequence of transforming the other into a non-subject, an empty locus or passive receptacle for whatever constructions the philosopher may place upon it. Thus, in Derrida's words,

> [t]he profundity of the empiricist intention must be recognized beneath the naiveté of certain of its historical expressions. It is the *dream* of a purely *heterological* thought at its source. A *pure* thought of *pure* difference . . . By radicalizing the theme of the infinite exteriority of the other, Levinas thereby assumes the aim which has more or less secretly animated all the philosophical gestures which have been called *empiricisms* in the history of philosophy.

The point can be made (as by Derrida here) through an intricate reading of Levinas's texts that draws out their 'unthought axiomatics', and which moreover – in quasi-Kantian mode – demonstrates the 'conditions of impossibility' that arise to complicate his thinking. But it can also be stated more simply in the form of a straightforward appeal to reflective self-evidence. Thus the 'other' can exert no claim upon us as sentient, thinking, and willing subjects if their otherness extends so far – or goes so deep – as to place them (for all that we can possibly know) in a wholly different realm of being and experience.

It seems to me that Derrida's essay on Levinas contains some crucial (though hitherto neglected) implications for present-day critical theory. This neglect is not so much a matter of indifference – since the past few years have seen a marked growth of interest in Derrida, Levinas, and the 'ethics of deconstruction' – as a tendency to focus on his subsquent (1987) essay which in many ways constitutes a gesture of atonement, or at any rate adopts a less critical stance with regard to the central philosophic issues.[104] Thus Derrida asks, among other things, how it is that Levinas can treat the question of gender-marking in ethical discourse as a matter of subsidiary concern, one that can always be subsumed or effaced before the deeper (strictly primordial) question of ethics as the recognition of absolute alterity. Thus he (Derrida) continues to interrogate the 'conditions of (im)possibility' for Levinas's project, though now through a mode of appreciative commentary that acknowledges the profound significance of that project while criticizing only its localized blind-spots of cultural presupposition. Most recent commentators (Critchley among them) have taken it that this later text marks an advance, a development beyond the residual elements of 'critique' that marked the earlier essay, and hence a clear sign that deconstruction discovers its ultimate fulfilment in Levinas's thinking of an ethics beyond all the concepts and categories of Western epistemological thought. On this view the notion of *criticizing* Levinas – of showing, as Derrida previously put it, how '(b)y making the origin of language, meaning, and difference the relation to the infinitely other, Levinas is resigned to betraying his own intentions in his philosophical discourse' – can only indicate a lapse into pre-deconstructive (worse still: into Kantian-enlightenment) ways of thought.[105] On the contrary, I would argue: his earlier essay is by far the more cogent and penetrating piece of work, an essay that argues conclusively – whatever his subsequent shift of tack – that the modish thematics of 'otherness' and radical 'difference' can amount to no more than a species of well-intentioned but ultimately incoherent and self-deceiving rhetoric.

VI

'The dream of a purely heterological thought . . .'

Let me now provide a focus for these various lines of argument by taking some examples from the field of contemporary cultural and literary studies. One context in which talk of the 'other' figures very prominently is that of the New Historicism, itself much influenced by Foucault's genealogies of power/knowledge and by other such projects (like that of Edward Said) designed to bring Western ethnocentric discourse up against the limits of its own self-assured conceptual and ethico-political mastery.[106] The typical New Historicist scene of instruction is one that goes roughly as follows. The emissary of Western culture – the explorer, colonial adventurer, New World settler, etc. – begins by treating 'native' habits of religious or cultural belief as mere priestly impostures, superstitious tokens of a primitive life-form which must now give way before the superior truth-claims (or, failing that, the subjugating force) of a 'civilized' Western discourse. But it can also happen – with more enquiring or sceptical minds – that this process takes a self-reflexive turn, leading them to ask whether maybe their own (e.g. Christian) habits of cultural belief might not be likewise the products of a hegemonic will-to-truth vested in certain localized interests of Church, state, or economic dominance. Hence – in very summary and simplified form – the phenomenon of so-called 'Renaissance scepticism', that underground movement of advanced or radical opinion whose emergence as a kind of incipient counter-public sphere Stephen Greenbalatt has lately done much to document.[107]

But there are several points that need making here as against the standard New Historicist account. First, this process could not have occurred – or scepticism have made any inroads on the currency of taken-for-granted belief – had the colonizers not treated *themselves and their native informants alike* as subjects with a shared human interest in dispelling the sources of illusion, attaining a better (more enlightened) grasp of the ideological mechanisms involved, and thereby extending the exercise of reason beyond its local (doctrinally sanctioned) limits. This is also to say (second point) that when Greenblatt and his fellow New Historicists invoke the 'other' – the colonial other – as both victim and subverter of Western hegemonic discourse, they cannot in all consistency maintain that rhetoric of 'absolute alterity' which would represent such otherness as altogether outside the range of our own (not to mention the colonizers') knowledge and experience. And third, such arguments presuppose the existence of truth-seeking (knowledge-constitutive) interests which form both an intersubjective, trans-cultural horizon of shared understanding and a link between cognitive and ethical orders of discourse. That is, they cannot help but invoke the values of enlightened critical thought, whatever the rhetoric currently deployed to debunk or discredit such values. For it is (once again) a condition of doing justice to the marginalized 'other' that we should strive so far as possible to establish the relevant historical facts, to understand what forces were mobilized to the end of suppressing or distorting those facts, and to perceive the other – in Derrida's words – as an 'alter ego' with equivalent interests in the sphere of justice and truth. None of which would be remotely possible if such encounters took place in the featureless zone of a textualized 'history' where self and other are reduced to mere oppositional terms in an abstract economy of difference.

Here, as so often in contemporary theory, what we witness is a wholesale transference of linguistic (more precisely: of Saussurian) models and metaphors into a realm where their pertinence is, to say the least, open to question. The first such fallacy is that which consists in extending a structural–synchronic model of the sign – the binary logic of an 'arbitrary' relation between signifier and signified – to those higher-level units of discourse (the sentence and beyond) at which quite other terms of analysis apply, among them propositional criteria of truth and falsehood and issues of speaker's intent.[108] The second, following directly from this, is the notion that subjectivity is constituted wholly in or through language, with the upshot (eagerly embraced by post-structuralists) that nothing exists – no possible appeal to truth, knowledge, experience, or judgment – beyond the henceforth all-encompassing field of discursive or textual representations. It is not hard to see how the current talk of 'otherness', 'absolute alterity', and the like appears the only option for those who espouse this line but who still wish to claim some ethical basis for their work. Given such premises the conclusion can scarcely be denied. If subjectivity is an epiphenomenon of language, and if languages differ so radically in respect of their criteria for truth, logic, rational argument, consistency of judgment etc., then indeed there is no choice but to treat other subjects as utterly opaque to all our good-willed efforts at mutual comprehension. Postmodernist ethics can thus be seen as making a virtue of this self-imposed necessity, or in effect raising bafflement to a high point of moral principle. But of course there is another way of looking at all this. For if the premises are wrong – based on a reductive and hugely over-generalized model of linguistic understanding – then there is no good reason (aside from predisposed bias) to draw the ultra-sceptical conclusion.[109]

This is the great fudged issue of contemporary cultural theory, or at least those strains of it deriving from post-structuralism and kindred sources. With the New Historicists, like Foucault before them, the normative dimension is everywhere manifest in their will to redeem the long history of oppression inflicted upon subject peoples, sexual minorities, 'deviant' sub-groups, victims of coercive (psychiatric or penal) institutions, etc. Yet their theorizing offers absolutely no basis for any such principled ethical stance. Indeed, it cuts away the very grounds of judgment by asserting that history is entirely a product of textual or discursive representation, that subjects are likewise constructed in language (along with all categories of knowledge and experience), and hence – as Lyotard would have it – that we commit a wrong, an infraction of the narrative differend, by presuming to speak on the other's behalf, or by invoking ideas of truth and justice that would somehow transcend this condition of absolute alterity. Hence the current high vogue for invocations of the Kantian sublime, that figure of ultimate 'heterogeneity' (Lyotard again) which supposedly signals the unbridgeable gulf between cognitive and evaluative phrase-genres, or the impossibility that judgments could ever be harmonized in a *sensus communis* of inter-subjective values and truth-seeking interests.[110] (Understandably these theorists ignore or play down what Kant has to say about the beautiful, since it is here that he provides a countervailing stress on precisely those values and interests.)[111] Hence also – as I have noted

– the attitude that raises 'otherness' into a kind of transcendental shibboleth, a term whose deployment very often serves as a peremptory conversation-stopper, a routine rebuke to anyone who broaches substantive ethical and political issues.

Thus for instance it is taken as a sign of cultural arrogance – of a lingering attachment to Enlightenment beliefs – if Western commentators presume to criticize aspects of Islamic fundamentalism, among them (where evidence exists) the return to cruel forms of physical punishment, the drive to impose archaic and repressive codes of conduct for women, and the persecuting zeal towards dissident (i.e. liberal or secular) movements of thought. There are two main reasons – so it is argued – why such criticism always and inevitably falls into a posture of sheer bad faith. One has to do with the critic's belonging to a different (incommensurable) 'form of life' whose constitutive values and presuppositions are such as to prevent any genuine understanding of the cultural practice in question. This is the line of counter-argument common to Wittgensteinian, communitarian, and sundry postmodernist thinkers. The other objection is more in the nature of a moral *tu quoque*, since it rests on the claim – no doubt justified up to a point – that Western intellectuals are in no strong position to adopt this elevated stance, since their own pre-history is tainted by all manner of brutal and intolerant practices, including those forms of exported (colonial or imperial) violence which were often accompanied by just such a rhetoric of high-toned civilizing purpose. It would be stupid to ignore the force of this charge, given the quantity of evidence gathered in the writing of critics such as Edward Said, as well as the everyday witness of events like the Gulf War and other neo-colonialist exploits.[112] All the same there is a difference – a crucial difference – between acknowledging this burden of historical responsibility and taking it as pretext for a wholesale rejection of Enlightenment values and beliefs. Indeed these two responses are mutually exclusive if the latter is pursued to its current (postmodernist) extreme. For such acknowledgment can come about only through that joint process of historical enquiry, of ethical reflection and self-directed cultural critique which the Enlightenment inherited from Montaigne, Spinoza and others in the same emancipatory tradition, and whose fortunes are now inextricably bound up with the 'unfinished project of modernity'.[113]

Of course this argument would cut little ice with a postmodern sceptic like Lyotard, one for whom a mere listing of events over the past two centuries – wars, revolutions, counter-revolutions, the whole sorry spectacle to date – is warrant enough for dismissing that project as the merest of transient illusions.[114] And no doubt there are reasons nearer home (among them the melancholy wisdom of hindsight prevalent in the post-1968 generation of French intellectuals) which have also left their mark. One might respond by recalling Gramsci's words – 'pessimism of the intellect, optimism of the will' – set down at a time, and in personal circumstances, far worse than anything confronted by these present-day thinkers. But one could also point out the philosophical confusions, notably the angled misreadings of Kant, that lead them on the one hand to treat the sublime as a master-trope of radical heterogeneity, driving a wedge between the cognitive and evaluative orders of discourse, and on the other – at the opposite extreme – to construe the record (the evidential witness) of past and present events as a standing rebuke to enlightened ideas of reason, truth, and social justice.[115] What this betokens is a failure to engage adequately with thinkers in the 'other' tradition of critical theory, that which runs (broadly speaking) from Kant to Habermas, and which figures for postmodernists like Lyotard only as a pretext for highly selective or revisionist readings.[116] The result, as I have argued, is to promulgate a range of quasi-radical ideas – philosophy as just another 'kind of writing', history as likewise a textual or fictive construct, ethics as the encounter with an 'absolute alterity' conceived on the structuralist model of linguistic difference – which work to undermine every last prospect of enlightened human understanding.

That these ideas have come to occupy the high ground of 'advanced' theoretical debate is all the more disturbing in light of contemporary real-world social and political events. In a previous book (*Uncritical Theory: postmodernism, intellectuals and the Gulf War*) I argued that such thinking might well bring comfort to the ideologues, propagandists, and media pundits.[117] After all, what could better suit their purposes than the message that fact and fiction are wholly indistinguishable, that truth is purely and simply a product of consensus belief, and moreover that the 'other' as perceived by us – from the viewpoint, say, of a 'New World Order' equated with Western hegemonic interests – must either conform to our own preconceptions or be considered so utterly (unredeemably) alien as to inhabit a realm quite beyond the sphere of civilized 'democratic' life. Such was indeed the line promoted by Gulf War apologists like Francis Fukuyama, along with a range of auxilliary themes – the 'end of ideology (and/or history)', the New World Order, the demise of Enlightenment values, etc. – which chimed happily with the current postmodernist wisdom.[118] What Fukuyama had to say about the 'Iraqs and Ruritanias' of this world – that they must henceforth be consigned, regretfully but firmly, to the dustbin of history – reads like a grim flipside variant of postmodern talk about radical 'otherness'. One need only consider the events unfolding, as I write, in ex-Yugoslavia and portions of the erstwhile Soviet bloc to see how easily such thinking can translate into the worst forms of ethnic prejudice and collective paranoia. For it is no great distance, whether in philosophic or in psychological terms, from the attitude that on principle renounces all claim to know or comprehend the other to the attitude that views otherness as a threat – an absolute since radically alien threat – to its own very being and life-world.

One can therefore see why Derrida, in his early essay on Levinas, should have thought it important to criticize such thinking, to question its conditions of possibility, despite what is clearly a sympathetic reading in many respects. Few thinkers can have had more cause than Derrida – born to Sephardic Jewish parents in French-occupied Algeria, and growing up during the worst years of antisemitic prejudice – to reflect on the complex imbrications of national identity and ethnic or cultural difference.[119] Nor need one commit any kind of reductive 'biographical fallacy' in suggesting that this background has a pointed relevance to aspects of his ethical and political thought. For as I argued above in relation to philosophy of science there is nothing inconsistent about pursuing an interest in the so-called 'context of discovery' – in matters of circumstance, life-history, personal motivation, and the like – while also respecting the 'context of justification' as the realm wherein arguments or truth-claims are subject to more rigorous evaluative norms. Thus when Derrida reads Levinas he does so on the one hand with a view to the latter's situation as a Jewish philosopher writing out of a knowledge and experience of the Holocaust, and on the other – as always in his finest work – with a strict regard to philosophic protocols of logic, consistency, and truth. Moreover, in so far as he criticizes Levinas, it is because the latter's idea of ethics as a discourse of radical alterity would in effect close off the very prospect of any such intersubjective appeal to the other's knowledge and experience. Thus: '(t)he other as alter ego signifies the other as other, irreducible to *my* ego, precisely because it is an ego, because it has the form of an ego. The egoity of the other permits him to say "ego" as I do; and this is why he is Other, and not a stone, or a being without speech in my *real economy*' (Derrida's emphases).[120] To treat the other as radically and absolutely other would amount, he argues, to a kind of empiricist (or phenomenalist) reduction, a gesture that goes so far towards acknowledging his or her claims to autonomous being that it ends up by repeating philosophy's oldest, most spontaneous gesture of exclusion. Such, we recall, is 'the dream of a purely *heterological* thought, a *pure* thought of *pure* difference . . . We say the *dream* because it must vanish at daybreak, as soon as language reawakens.'[121] This is why Levinas, as Derrida reads him, is 'resigned to betraying his own intentions in his philosophical discourse'. Simply to raise these questions in language – and even more so in a language whose resources inescapably derive to a very great extent from the tradition of Western post-Hellenic thought – is enough to deflect Levinas's project from its overt or avowed intent. Derrida's point (and what distinguishes, in his words, a deconstructive reading from a straightforward 'critique in the Enlightenment style') is that Levinas's texts themselves provide all the evidence of his being too perceptive, too intelligent and good-willed a thinker to fall into the more facile varieties of postmodern counter-enlightenment talk. It is the same generous and principled acknowledgment that Derrida makes when he reads the texts of Plato, Rousseau, Husserl, and Lévi-Strauss as revealing a complexity of motive and intent beyond anything that would register on a direct appeal to what the author manifestly had in mind.[122] Nor is this merely a 'principle of charity' – or an optimizing strategy of thought – that tries to make the best of otherwise recalcitrant material. For it is Derrida's contention (and the most profound wager in all his work) that to reflect upon these questions with sufficient understanding of their historical, ethical, and philosophic pertinence is *necessarily* to reveal the blind-spots of a discourse – whether that of philosophy or anti-philosophy, enlightenment or counter-enlightenment – which seeks to exclude some feared or rejected other. It is the mark of his respect for Levinas's thinking (for its rightful but not absolute or radical otherness) that he credits such thinking with an order of insight attainable only through the dialogue of minds, cultures, and traditions which *ex hypothese* it appears to deny.

'Are we Greeks? Are we Jews?', Derrida asks in the closing paragraph of 'Violence and Metaphysics'. 'We live in the difference
between the Jew and the Greek, which is perhaps what is called
history.'[123] This passage refers us back to the essay's epigraph, taken
from Matthew Arnold's *Culture and Anarchy*, where the same question is raised in a speculative form which again – as with Derrida –
asserts the need for sustained dialogue while deferring the appeal to
any premature (Hegelian) overcoming of otherness and difference.
'Hellenism and Hebraism', Arnold writes: 'between these two points
of influence moves our world. At one time it feels more powerfully
the attraction of one of them, at another time of the other, and it
ought to be, though it never is, evenly and happily balanced between
them.'[124] In Arnold, though Derrida forbears to make the point, this
rhetoric of fine even-handedness is soon belied by an argument that
one-sidedly promotes the culture of Hellenic 'sweetness and light'
while equating its Judaic (or Judaeo-Christian) counterpart with
everything that Arnold finds to criticize in the civilization of his day.
To this extent *Culture and Anarchy* may be read as an instance of
precisely that Hellenizing impulse – that elevation of 'disinterested'
knowledge and truth over the ethical claims of unmediated otherness
– which Levinas calls into question. 'All the classical concepts inter-
rogated by Levinas are thus dragged toward the *agora*, summoned to
justify themselves in an ethico-political language that they have not
always sought – or believed that they sought – to speak, summoned
to transpose themselves into this language by confessing their violent
aims.'[125] But again one notes in this passage a twofold complicating
emphasis: its reminder of the violence that can always go along with
such ethical 'interrogation' of violence, and its suggestion that those
'classical concepts' may themselves provoke a deeper, more sustained self-questioning than Levinas attributes to them.

Here it is worth recalling Derrida's criticism of Foucault for laying
claim to a language of absolute alterity – one that would inhabit the
very element of madness – while the mere fact of writing a book
about madness, a reasoned and consequent discourse on the topic, is
enough to refute that claim. For the other side of Foucault's error is
his will to play down the 'audacity' of the Cartesian *cogito*, indeed its
'mad audacity', that which drives it to confront the most extreme
imaginable threats to the composure of philosophic reason. Perhaps,
Derrida ventures, 'we (like Foucault) are too well assured of our-

selves and too well accustomed to the framework of the Cogito, rather than to the critical experience of it'.[126] What this has to say about the relation between reason and its 'other' (or philosophy and ethics) can best be brought out by juxtaposing two passages from Derrida's essays on Foucault and Levinas. Thus:

> [b]y virtue of the historical enunciation through which philosophy tranquilizes itself and excludes madness, philosophy also betrays itself (or betrays itself as thought), enters a crisis and a forgetting of itself that are an essential and necessary period of its movement. I philosophize only *in terror*, but in the *confessed* terror of going mad. The confession is simultaneously, at its present moment, oblivion and unveiling, protection and exposure: economy.[127]

With which compare the following from 'Violence and Metaphysics', a passage that likewise rejects the possibility of broaching an ethics 'outside' or 'beyond' the resources of Greek conceptuality, but which also denies – as in Derrida's rejoinder to Foucault – that such dependence is in any way a tranquil, a placid or a self-reassuring affair. 'The entirety of philosophy', Derrida writes, 'is conceived on the basis of its Greek source.' What is more,

> [t]his amounts neither to an occidentalism, nor to an historicism . . . That Plato, for Husserl, was the founder of a reason and a philosophical task whose telos was still sleeping in the shadows; or that for Heidegger, on the contrary, Plato marks the moment at which the thought of Being forgets itself and is determined as philosophy – this difference is decisive only at the culmination of a common root which is Greek . . . At a historical depth which the sciences and philosophies of history can only presuppose, we know that we are consigned to the security of the Greek element; and we know it with a knowledge and a confidence which are neither habitual nor comfortable but, on the contrary, permit us to experience torment or distress in general.[128]

We may now understand how this 'element' that Derrida refers to is neither 'occidental' (i.e. the perquisite of some vaguely defined 'Western metaphysics'), nor just the product of a naive historicism that equates its own values of reason and truth with the unfolding of some grand world-historical destiny. Rather, it is the element outside of which no thinking can occur, even (and especially) those kinds of thinking that strive to transcend the more limited contexts of localized cultural belief. For it is impossible to conceive how this should come about in the absence of certain conditions – conditions of mutual intelligibility – which provide the only means of interpreting 'otherness' as anything more than a catch-all slogan. That is to say, these gestures toward a politics of difference (or an ethics of radical alterity) remain ineffectual so long as they are couched at this level of abstract generality. What they lack – in common with much postmodern and post-structuralist thought – is any notion of the subject (the knowing, willing, judging and experiencing subject) that could bear such a weight of ethical argument.

This is why Derrida, despite his detailed reservations with regard to Husserlian phenomenology, none the less sees fit to defend that project from the charge brought against it by Levinas. Deconstruction may go very far in the questioning of Husserl's more problematical claims, his reliance on an 'unthought axiomatics' of speech as self-presence and primordial intuition.[129] But Derrida's readings leave no doubt that he regards these problems as essential – indeed inescapable – for any philosophy that is not to collapse into naive psychologism on the one hand, or formalist abstraction on the other. Such is the perpetual oscillation, as Derrida describes it, that marks Husserl's thinking at its moments of greatest rigour, and which also (contrary to Levinas's strictures) keeps open the constant interrogative exchange between structure and genesis, form and meaning, epistemology and ethics. If 'a certain structuralism has always been philosophy's most spontaneous gesture', then equally 'it is always something like an *opening* that will frustrate the structuralist project'.[130] Thus Husserl, in Derrida's words,

had to navigate between the Scylla and Charybdis of logicizing structuralism and psychologistic geneticism . . .He had to open up a new direction of philosophical attention and permit the discovery of a concrete, but nonempirical, intentionality, a 'transcendental experience' that would be 'constitutive', that is, like all intentionality, simultaneously productive and revelatory, active and passive.[131]

That this project in some sense 'failed' – that it gave rise to insoluble antinomies or aporias in Husserl's thought – is for Derrida (unlike some of his disciples) no reason to regard phenomenology as a closed chapter in the history of thought. On the contrary: it is here that philosophy discovers both its innermost vocation and the challenge of that 'otherness' which, *pace* Levinas, emerges (or finds an answering voice) only through the kind of reflective dialogue that philosophy seeks to promote.

I say '*pace* Levinas' not in the commonplace (near meaningless) sense of that phrase but with reference to Derrida's precise articulation of the issue between them. 'Are we Greeks? Are we Jews? But who, we?' And again, in the closing passage of his essay:

> To what horizon of peace does the language which asks this question belong? From whence does it draw the energy of its question? Can it account for the historical *coupling* of Judaism and Hellenism? And what is the meaning of the *copula* in this proposition from the most Hegelian of modern novelists: 'Jewgreek is Greekjew. Extremes meet'?[132]

This allusion to Joyce's *Ulysses* provides a neat symmetry with the epigraph from Arnold that I cited above. But more than that, it evokes a large background of associated argument – especially in Derrida's essay 'The Supplement of Copula' – bearing on the issue of cultural alterity and the question how far we can intelligibly claim that different languages (or conceptual schemes) entail different modes of perception, knowledge, or ontological commitment.[133] The gist of that essay – to summarize very crudely – is that relativist thinkers, the linguist Emile Benveniste among them, who assert the priority of language over thought (or linguistics over philosophy) are unable to state their case without presupposing the ubiquity of the copula as that which makes possible every form of predicative judgment or assertion.[134] There is perhaps no need to remark once again how close is the resemblance between Derrida's argument and those advanced by philosophers like Putnam and Davidson. Of course they go very different ways around in arriving at this similar conclusion. Derrida typically presents his case through a lengthy and meticulous deconstructive reading of Husserl, Levinas, Benveniste, and other thinkers in the broadly 'Continental' tradition. Davidson and Putnam proceed by a shorter route, one that raises issues of 'radical translation' and the minimal requirements for what should count as understanding a language. But they all three converge on the central point: that there exist *a priori* conditions of intelligibility which must be thought of as characterizing not some particular but *any possible* human language.

'On this matter', Derrida writes, 'no analysis will either circumvent or exclude the tribunal of Aristotelianism.'[135] The reference here is to Aristotle's table of the categories, or forms of predicative judgment, which supposedly comprise an exhaustive inventory of reason or thinking in general, quite apart from its localized instantiation in this or that natural language.[136] For Benveniste, on the contrary, this 'little document' merely goes to show how Aristotle (and numerous philosophers after him) had erected a wholesale, quasi-transcendental metaphysics and ontology on a linguistic function – the copula – which pertained only to the Greek and kindred languages, and whose presumed universality was merely an artefact of their own parochial viewpoint. But how can this be? Derrida asks. More specifically: what can be Benveniste's justification for treating as a merely contingent fact about this or that natural language the capacity of language to raise such questions with regard to its own status *vis-à-vis* the categories of thought and judgment? 'Is it not strange to qualify as empirical the necessity of an expression, the necessity to bring the conceivable to statement in a given language?'[137] Here again – as so often with Derrida – it is a matter of demonstrating the conditions of *im*possibility that prevent a thinker from consistently maintaining that which s/he quite expressly sets out to maintain. In Benveniste's case, the resultant aporias are such as necessarily 'engage anyone who takes on the task of defining the constraints which limit philosophical discourse; for it is from the latter that the noncritical notions that are applied to its delimitation must be borrowed'.[138] In short it is impossible to venture a single proposition concerning the order of priority between language and thought without, in the process, invoking one or other of those categories that Aristotle laid down in his 'little document'.

Thus: '(t)he notion of a linguistic *system*, even if opposed to the notions of logical system, or system of categories, and even if one attempted to reduce the latter to the former, would never have been possible outside the history (and) of the concepts of metaphysics as theory, *epistēmē* etc.'[139] Benveniste effectively concedes as much when *on the one hand* he argues (in company with ethno-linguistic philosophers like B. L. Whorf) that all truth-claims, ontologies, metaphysical postulates etc. are ultimately 'relative to language', and *on the other* presents the argument for this supposed fact of cultural relativity in a language that draws – necessarily so – on categorical (translinguistic) criteria of truth and validity.[140] 'Everything happens', Derrida writes, 'as if the general problem had nothing specifically Aristotelian about it, as if it were not essentially linked to the history indicated by the name of "Aristotle" or of his "heritage".'[141] Such would be the case if Benveniste could find some other language that got along without the promiscuous range of functions (copulative, predicative, ontological) which are subsumed under the verb 'to be' in ancient Greek and its latterday cognates. For this purpose, Benveniste remarks, one should select a language 'of an entirely different type to compare with the Greek, because it is precisely in the internal organization of their categories that linguistic types differ the most'.[142] And indeed he claims to do just that by taking as his example the Ewe language (spoken in the Togo region) where the various functions are 'divided among several verbs'. What such instances prove (or so it might seem) is that there is nothing in the nature of reality, reason, or truth that underwrites Aristotle's categories, but only the habit – endemic among philosophers – of erecting large metaphysical claims on the basis of contingent linguistic facts.

But Derrida's argument still holds, as can be seen if one enquires (like Davidson on Whorf) into the conditions of possibility for comparing languages in point of their divergent ontologies or conceptual schemes. 'What resources of translation are put to work here? Benveniste asks this question himself; but in disqualifying his own description as "a bit contrived", he does not wonder how such a contrivance is possible and why it is not totally absurd or inoperable.'[143] Just as Whorf, on Davidson's account, uses English to characterize a language (Hopi Indian) that purportedly cannot be 'calibrated' with English, so Benveniste seeks to define what is different about Ewe – its lack of ontological categories predicated on the verb 'to be' – in a language that not only deploys those resources itself but also (necessarily) imputes them to Ewe. For as Derrida notes, '[t]he absence of "to be", the absence of this singular lexeme, is absence itself. In general, is not the semantic value of *absence* dependent on the lexical-semantic value of "to be"?'[144] By an intrinsic necessity of language – one whose conditions can be formalized or stated in strictly *a priori* (that is to say, categorical) terms – Benveniste is compelled to admit the existence of trans-linguistic categories. From which it follows that one cannot simply relativize ontology to the inherited forms, the lexical resources or grammatico-semantic structures of some particular (in this case ancient Greek) language. For '(w)ithout the transcategoriality of "to be" . . . the transition between categories of language and categories of thought would not have been possible, either in the one sense or the other, for Aristotle or for Benveniste'.[145]

Philosophy is in this sense 'before' linguistics, its conceptual resources always presupposed in whatever the linguist has to say concerning the relation (or the order of priority) between language and thought. But to advance such a claim is not to go in for the kind of disciplinary one-upmanship that would grant philosophy the status of a master-discourse *vis-à-vis* the regional sciences of linguistics, ethnography, cultural criticism, etc. Nor is it to argue – as might be inferred from Derrida's critique of Benveniste – that *one particular* tradition of philosophy, the post-Hellenic tradition that descends from Plato to Husserl, is likewise privileged by virtue of possessing some ultimate (categorical or metalinguistic) access to knowledge and truth. 'Is there a "metaphysics" outside the Indo-European organization of the function "to be"?'[146] This is not, Derrida says, 'in the least an ethnocentric question'. It would be so only if taken to imply that cultures laying claim to a heritage of 'metaphysical' thought were thereby marked out as superior, or again (the vulgar-deconstructionist variant) that such cultures were revealed as being in the grip of naive 'logocentric' concepts and values. Both responses presume the possibility of conceiving some language *without* metaphysics, one that would be either pre-metaphysical (as not having yet advanced to that stage of philosophic or reflective maturity) or post-metaphysical (as having somehow – with benefit of deconstructive insight – moved decisively beyond it). From both points of view Derrida's question might appear 'ethnocentric', whether to the advantage or to the disadvantage of so-called 'Western metaphysics'. However, if properly understood, that question 'does not amount to envisaging that other languages might be *deprived* of the surpassing mission of philosophy and metaphysics but, on the contrary, avoids projecting outside the West very determined forms of "history" and "culture" '.[147] For it is precisely by relativizing issues of knowledge and truth – counting them internal to this or that 'history' or 'culture' – that ethnocentrism first gets a hold. And this applies, as we have seen, to any version of the argument (whether New Historicist, feminist, neopragmatist, Levinasian, postmodernist, or whichever) that raises the ethics or the politics of 'otherness' into a high point of abstract principle.

VII

Textual encounters: the prison-house of 'discourse'

'Jewgreek is Greekjew. Extremes meet.' When Derrida closes his essay on Levinas with the cryptic citation from *Ulysses* it is not just a routine pacifying gesture, and even less – despite his allusion to Joyce as 'the most Hegelian of modern novelists' – a dialectical ruse that aims to transcend the difference between them, and hence to give Derrida the last word. Rather, his point is that 'extremes meet' on the ground of a mutual intelligibility which belongs to the nature of intersubjective experience and which is presupposed by every attempt to articulate an ethics of other-regarding principle. Such thinking may encounter manifold problems of communicative grasp, but in its absence the 'other' must remain just that, an alien (and potentially threatening) *object* of thought, as distinct from a human *alter ego* with thoughts, desires, and ethical interests recognizably akin to one's own.

Of course it may be said that Derrida goes a very long and complicated way around in reaching this (somewhat obvious) conclusion. After all, doesn't it stand to reason – from any but a bother-headed deconstructionist viewpoint – that one's ethical comportment will very largely depend on the capacity to place oneself in the other's position, to appreciate the difficulties that often arise in situations of moral choice, and thus to treat others on the basis of a tolerant yet principled regard for the conflicts of priority and interest involved? If philosophers have anything useful to contribute then they had surely better take at least that much for granted – without all the specialized detours *via* epistemology, phenomenology, hermeneutics, and so forth – as a matter of plain self-evidence. In which case it might seem that Derrida is labouring the point when he deploys such wire-drawn subtleties of argument to establish that the 'other' is indeed an *alter ego*, and not (*pace* Levinas) the locus of an 'absolute alterity' which requires the willing suspension of all 'egological' categories.

But this is to ignore both the specificity of Derrida's work – its philosophical pertinence – and the way that these specialized issues engage with questions of an ethico-political import well beyond the confines of current theoretical debate. For as I have argued already it is no coincidence that 'otherness' has become such a live topic among critical intellectuals at a time when the old power-blocs are crumbling, when any hopes for a 'New World Order' have receded under the strain of resurgent nationalist strife, and when the rhetoric of difference often goes along with a drive to assert the most atavistic forms of ethnic or racial identity. Nor is it surprising that at least a few of those thinkers – among them (notably) some erstwhile proponents of 'textuality' as the marker of cultural difference – have lately shown signs of shifting ground towards a more 'enlightenment' position.

Thus in his book *Culture and Imperialism* (1992) Edward Said remarks that '(a) new and in my opinion appalling tribalism is fracturing societies, separating peoples, promoting greed, bloody conflict, and uninteresting assertions of minor ethnic or group particularity'.[148] And some three hundred pages on – but I think with the same consideration in mind – he has this to say about Toussaint L'Ouverture and the Santo Domingo slave uprising, as narrated in C. L. R. James's classic *The Black Jacobins*.[149] 'James writes of Toussaint', Said writes of James,

> as someone who takes up the struggle for human freedom – a struggle going on in the metropolis to which culturally he owes his language and many of his moral allegiances . . . He appropriates the principles of the Revolution not as a black man but as a human, and he does so with a dense historical awareness of how in finding the language of Diderot, Rousseau and Robespierre one follows predecessors creatively, using the same words, employing inflections that transformed rhetoric into actuality.[150]

I hardly need stress – for readers familiar with his work – how great is the distance between Said's attitude toward Enlightenment values, as declared in this passage, and the stance adopted in previous books like *Orientalism, Covering Islam*, and *The World, the Text and the Critic*.[151] In part this has to do with his growing recognition of the harms inflicted by that 'new and appalling tribalism', that doctrine of ethnic and racial difference which is currently wreaking such bloody havoc in numerous regions of the world. But it also marks a significant shift of theoretical perspective with regard to the issue of truth, meaning, and textual representation. In those earlier books Said aligned himself closely with Foucault – and implicitly with the New Historicists – by arguing that 'truth' is a discursive construct, a function of the various languages, narratives, or power/knowledge differentials that determine what shall count as veridical utterance at any given time.[152] Thus the business of the critical intellectual is no longer (as it was for those deluded 'enlightenment' types) to speak up for truth and the universal values of ethico-political justice, as against the forces of ignorance, prejudice, ideological 'false consciousness', and so forth. Rather, it is to expose the power-seeking interests that mask behind every such rhetoric of enlightenment, every such attempt to monopolize the discourse of reason, principle, and virtue.

In which case the critic of Western 'orientalism' will need to apply a certain self-denying ordinance when it comes to contesting the falsehoods and stereotypes put about by scholars, historians, anthropologists, journalists, foreign relations 'experts', and the like. For there can be no question – if s/he is to avoid the obvious *tu quoque* rejoinder – of treating those ideas as false, mendacious, ideologically motivated, or determined merely by forms of unthinking cultural prejudice. To argue like this would be to fall straight back into that old 'enlightenment' ideology whose besetting vice was to mistake its own agenda of culture-specific values and beliefs for a universal discourse of justice and truth. So the best that the critic can do in these circumstances is produce some alternative – more rhetorically efficacious – set of images, narratives and representations which aim to displace the authorized *doxa* through a strategy of strong-revisionist textual engagement. But nobody who has read *Orientalism* or *Covering Islam* could come away believing this to be the limit of Said's ambition in those works. As with Foucault there is a glaring discrepancy between the ethical passion – the passion for truth and justice – with which Said argues his case, and his refusal (in theory) to provide any normative justification for adopting that adversarial stance. One can see well enough how this came about, given Said's Foucauldian line on the ubiquitous workings of power/knowledge, his view of textuality (or discourse) as the field wherein those workings are most visibly manifest, and – until now – his express belief that the Enlightenment was a wholly Eurocentric affair, a discourse whose dark side was its massive indifference to the brutal facts of imperial aggression and colonial exploitation. Not that this charge-sheet had in any way diminished by the time Said completed his work toward *Culture and Imperialism*. But in two respects at least – historical and ethico-political – that work bears witness to a real transformation of attitude. The first (as shown by the passage on Toussaint, cited above) is Said's willingness to extend 'Enlightenment' as a historical term beyond its original European context to those other emancipatory movements – like the Santo Domingo revolt – that were able to invoke kindred ideas of *universal* liberty, justice, and human rights. From which it follows that such ideas are not simply (as Foucault would have it) a product of the omnipresent will-to-truth that translates into a hegemonic will-to-power. Nor are they – in the current textualist idiom – mere 'representations' (or strategies for shaping the narrative-discursive field) which possess no validity outside or beyond the moment of encounter between critic and text. The result of such thinking is a form of methodological solipsism, one that Said could never have embraced on account of his ethical commitment to the victims of injustice, untruth, and misrepresentation, but which he is now (with good reason) more anxious to repudiate. It can be seen most plainly in the New Historicist tendency to reduce everything – issues of truth, history, politics, ethics, cultural 'otherness' etc. – to this same dead level of textualized 'negotiation' where meaning, as Stanley Fish has adroitly pointed out, can be only a product of the critic's choice among the going range of options in this or that present-day 'interpretive community'.[153] Hence also New Historicism's curious mixture of a radical (or at least strong-revisionist) rhetoric with a certain pervasive bleakness of historical and political vision. As with Foucault, this derives from the conviction that subjects are always and everywhere caught up in a network of discourses – or power/knowledge differentials – beyond their capacity to comprehend or to change through any kind of knowing and willed intervention.

What is thus played out in New Historicist readings – in the 'moment of encounter' between critic and text – is that same deep blankness, that failure to recognize the other as an *alter ego*, which the critic imputes to those colonial adventurers and emissaries of Western 'civilization' confonted with the evidence of cultural difference in the form of 'native' practices, values, and beliefs. Stephen Greenblatt's essay 'Invisible Bullets' is perhaps the most striking case in point.[154] It offers some intriguing conjectures as to the psychodynamics of Renaissance scepticism, or the way that such colonial encounters produced a backlash of religious disbelief among at least some few free-thinking individuals or members of an advanced (mostly underground) intellectual culture. This involved a three-stage process of reasoning whose logic went roughly as follows. (1) It is our duty as believers in the true (Christian) faith to explain to these natives that their 'religions' are merely a species of priestly imposture, a means of enforcing obedience by conjuring up various imaginary bugbears. But (2) are these beliefs and techniques of enforcement – not to mention the resultant wars, persecution, and sectarian strife – *really* so different from those that prevail within the sphere of Western Christendom? Whence (3) the sceptical upshot: that perhaps Christianity is itself just a form of mass-induced irrational belief, a popular superstition maintained through various (more or less coercive) agencies, and one whose purpose, function, or effect is to blind subjects to the conditions of their own servitude.

Such was at any rate, in Greenblatt's reading, the conclusion arrived at by some thinkers on the radical (crypto-atheist) fringe of seventeenth-century debate. But what he won't for a moment entertain – in keeping with New Historicist precept – is the idea that this might actually have been an *enlightened and progressive* development of thought, as distinct from a purely reactive attitudinal formation. That is to say, Greenblatt will have no truck with a reading that would see in such episodes the emergence of a proto-enlightenment outlook, a capacity to put oneself in the other's place and thereby discover certain general truths about the sources of intolerance, injustice, and oppression along with the prospects – however remote – of ameliorating that shared condition. For Greenblatt (and likewise for Foucault) this could figure only as a woeful lapse into just those types of delusive binary opposition – truth/falsehood, knowledge/ignorance, progress/reaction, and so forth – which characterize Enlightenment as belonging irretrievably to the history of dead ideas. 'Textuality' thus functions for the New Historicists in much the same way that 'discourse' functions in Foucault's all-encompassing genealogies of power/knowledge. It serves as a kind of shorthand indicator for the idea that historical agency – like textual interpretation – is 'always already' inscribed in some pre-given system of differential power relations that allows of no alternative 'subject-position' (no access to 'knowledge' or 'truth') outside the currently existing field of discursive representations. So one can see why New Historicism, despite all its talk of cultural difference and alterity, nevertheless invites the charge of reducing those themes to the merest of rhetorical slogans. For if indeed it is the case, as these critics maintain, that textuality goes 'all the way down' – if there is nothing outside the endless play of recirculated meanings, representations, negotiative strategies, and textual *mises-en-scène* – then the 'other' can be nothing more than a construction out of this or that contemporary discourse.[155]

Hence the 'presentist' bias that several commentators, Elizabeth Fox-Genovese among them, have noted as a persistent liability in New Historicist writing.[156] The upshot is curiously akin to that strain of idealist thinking (derived from Hegel *via* F. H. Bradley) that allowed T. S. Eliot, in his essay 'Tradition and the Individual Talent', to treat mere history as a vulgar factical domain, a dimension transcended by the ideal order – the 'imaginary museum' of timeless masterpieces – which composed the great tradition of European literature.[157] And this despite New Historicism's quasi-materialist stress on the 'signifying practices', the discursive differentials and effects of power/knowledge that supposedly work to demystify any such naive transcendentalist vision. Small change, one might think, when the idiom shifts from a discourse of classical 'values' that circulate in a realm above and beyond all distinctions of historical time or place, to one that raises textuality (or a generalized 'economy of difference') to a point where it likewise effaces the distinction between past and present modes of knowledge and experience. In short, what this amounts to is a thoroughgoing (textualist) version of the 'hermeneutic circle'. If consistently applied it denies any access to history except by way of some local point of entry whose horizon is inescapably formed by present-day interpretive conventions or exegetical practices.

Foucault makes a virtue of grasping this particular nettle when he declares that all history is (or should be) a 'history of the present', a *wirkliche Geschichte* – in Nietzsche's phrase – aimed not so much towards establishing the truth of what actually occurred as towards the empowerment of thought and action through techniques of willed 'strong-revisionist' reading.[158] New Historicism takes a less combative line, committed as it is – in some respects at least – to the protocols of documentary scholarship and archival research. But these commitments count for little if the rhetoric of otherness – of cultural or temporal difference – goes along with a strain of deep-laid methodological solipsism, a conviction that such otherness must *both* be respected (in principle) as a locus of absolute alterity *and* (following Nietzsche) be interpreted in accordance with present-day values and priorities. Thus the New Historicists end up by impaling themselves on both horns of a false and artificial dilemma. Artificial, that is, in so far as it results from a needless (and philosophically confused) attempt to forgo any appeal to such 'enlightenment' notions as truth, knowledge, ethical agency, or the possibility of intersubjective (and hence trans-cultural) understanding. Nor are these confusions by any means confined to the realm of abstruse theoretical debate. For their real-world equivalent is to be found, as I have argued, in those instances of ethnic and nationalist conflict which also bear witness to the perilous linkage between notions of cultural difference-as-otherness and notions of cultural identity as that which defines itself over and against such otherness.

Here it is worth recalling Habermas's point: that present-day 'theory' (at least in its Francophile postmodern or post-structuralist forms) seems embarked upon a largely unwitting repetition of earlier episodes in the history of thought.[159] For this is not the first time that philosophy has been caught in the kind of chronically unstable oscillation (subject/object, self/other, identity/difference etc) which tends to develop during periods of intense ideological conflict or socio-political strain. Nowhere is this more apparent than in the dizzying succession of theses and counter-theses by which thinkers in the generation after Kant – Fichte, Schelling, Hegel, the romantic ironists and others – swung back and forth between the polar extremes of 'subjective' and 'objective' idealism.[160] One lesson that Habermas derives – in company with others like Manfred Frank – is the need for theorists to have some knowledge of this relevant pre-history if they are not to be drawn into a similar pattern of reactive, sterile, or deadlocked antithetical thinking.[161] Another is the argument (taken up by Habermas in his reflections on the subsequent course of German history) that such issues in the seemingly specialized sphere of philosophical debate may in fact have large – and potentially disastrous – implications beyond that sphere.[162] And the third lesson, inseparable from these, is that we need to keep faith with what Habermas calls the 'unfinished project of modernity', since it is only by thinking such issues through with the greatest possible lucidity and care that theory can avoid the constant danger of reverting to forms of unreflective pre-critical prejudice. In his view – to which I would very largely subscribe – this charge can be brought against many of those thinkers in the post-structuralist and affiliated camps who have raised the thematics of difference and alterity into a high point of mystified dogma.

The point is well made (albeit unintentionally) when Richard Rorty entitles one of his essays 'Nineteenth-Century Idealism and Twentieth-Century Textualism'.[163] In fact Rorty's purpose is to praise the latter movement for possessing the courage of its textualist convictions, for renouncing all ideas of truth, reason, interpretive fidelity etc., and for thus winning through to a 'strong-revisionist' standpoint never quite attained by its historical precursor. But the title takes on a more pointed negative significance in light of those failings and retrograde symptoms that Habermas remarks in the current post-structuralist recycling of idealist themes. It then becomes clear that, so far from representing an advance beyond that old (subject-centred or epistemological) paradigm, new textualism is a thoroughly regressive movement of thought, one that remains captive to the same antinomies without even perceiving this to be the case. Hence, as I have argued, its constant resort to a notional category of 'otherness' which becomes just a rhetorical place-filler, an empty locus that has to stand in for the absence of any ethics (or politics) worthy the name. For there is no other way that thinking can go once it is taken as read – according to the current post-structuralist *doxa* – that truth and reality are discursive constructs, that history is a product of narrative (or fictive) contrivance, and that the subject is likewise a transient epiphenomenon of language.[164] In which case our relationship with the 'other' comes down to a choice between treating him or her as an involuntary construction out of our own discourse, ideology, world-view, textual repertoire, or whatever, and at the opposite extreme (or so it might appear) refusing on principle to claim any knowledge – any common ground of insight or mutual understanding – that would infringe upon the other's right to be treated as a locus of absolute alterity. In fact these are not so much alternative positions as alternating aspects of the same false dilemma. On the textualist view – as dramatized most vividly in Greenblatt's 'Invisible Bullets' – the encounter with otherness must always take this form of a chronic oscillation between identity and difference, colonizer and colonized, the self and its other as binary terms in a network of relations (a 'general economy') analogous to that of language. What remains of the subject – the putative 'other' – is thus nothing more than a figment projected in the space of linguistic representation.

That this model has been extended so far beyond its legitimate (structural–synchronic) domain is a major cause of the confusions rife in present-day critical theory. But those confusions take on a much wider (and more ominous) import if one considers their meaning – their practical significance – in light of current world-political events. For if there is one harsh lesson that theorists should have learned from simply reading their daily newspapers over the past few years it is the fatal ease with which notions of ethnic and cultural 'difference' can be turned around and used to promote forms of racist or xenophobic sentiment. This may all seem worlds apart from the issues of epistemology, ethics, and philosophy of language so meticulously argued in Derrida's critique of Levinas. But the connection will appear less remote if one considers Levinas's case – his claim for the absolute priority of an ethics of otherness rooted in the tradition of Judaic moral and scriptural thought – with reference to recent events in Palestine and (more specifically) in the occupied territories of the West Bank and Gaza Strip. This is not the place – nor have I the authority – for any detailed discussion of the historical, ethical, and political issues involved. But there is a worse dereliction of responsibility that comes of believing (like many thinkers in the grip of cultural–relativist doctrine) that it is not for 'us' to reflect on the justice or injustice of Israeli government policy, given both 'our' (i.e. the British) record of strategic intervention in the region and – more generally – the wrong that we inflict by presuming to judge other people's concerns from a standpoint of 'enlightened' superior wisdom. For on this view there is simply no distinction to be drawn between the cultural–imperialist outlook that takes its own values for universal truths and the attempt – characteristic of Enlightenment thought – to respect the commonality of human interests while refusing such false (ethnocentric or partisan) visions of the common good.

This line of argument should be familiar enough to any reader who has followed me thus far. What it amounts to is another variant of the postmodern ethos – the doctrine of alterity, absolute difference, radical heterogeneity etc. – whose human implications and whose real-world consequences these theorists have scarcely begun to think through. Most often (as I have said) it starts out from an attitude of open-minded respect for the variety of cultural values and beliefs. But the endpoint is always a weak or strong version of the currently prevailing relativist line. In its weak (liberal–pluralist or communitarian) form this holds that since values are in some sense 'internal' to the language-game or life-form in question, therefore we should count ourselves unqualified to judge in matters beyond our own cultural purview. In the strong version – espoused by Levinas and implicit in much New Historicist writing – such good-willed pluralism is left far behind. It gives way to the quest for an ethics that would either fall silent in the face of absolute alterity, or represent it from the distance of a textual encounter which on principle renounces all claim to understanding beyond what present-day culture provides in the way of discourses, rhetorical strategies, narrative instances, and so forth. It is in this context, I suggest, that we should interpret Said's very marked change of outlook with regard to the 'discourse' of Enlightenment critique. For whatever its manifest shortcomings and failures to date – failures that Said has done as much as anyone to document – still it is the case that Enlightenment provides the only adequate resources (conceptual, ethical, and political) for reflecting on that same history.

VIII

Scepticism and Enlightenment:
Kristeva *contra* post-structuralism

Said is by no means alone in his movement away from the erswhile radical orthodoxy that equated truth, reason, and critique with the discourse of imperial oppression and which raised their counter-terms (textuality, difference, and otherness) to a high point of dissident principle. In two recent books by Julia Kristeva – *Strangers to Ourselves* and *Nations Without Nationalism* – one finds that orthodoxy called into question by one of its most influential exponents, a theorist who perhaps did more than anyone to establish the idea of 'signifying practice' as the royal road to social and political transformation.[165] I have room here only for a brief *resumée* of Kristeva's work in this field. Sufficient to say that her previous shifts of theoretical allegiance – roughly speaking, the post-1968 French trajectory from Marxism (or the primacy of class-politics) to psychoanalysis, feminism, and various forms of alternative radical engagement – were never such as to question the idea of *language* (textuality or representation) as the site where those struggles were most effectively carried on. This position is worked out in her book *The Revolution in Poetic Language*, itself a compendious re-statement of theses developed by the editorial collective of the journal *Tel Quel* during its period of high radical cachet in the late 1960s.[166] Along with a work like Barthes's *S/Z* – though without the same qualities of aphoristic brilliance and magpie theoretical eclecticism – it stands as a monument to those heady few years when the looked-for 'revolution' was at last to be ushered in through a discourse that denounced the repressive monological structures of the 'bourgeois realist text', that opened up the henceforth infinitized 'freeplay' of textual signification, and that offered the prospect of a new-found (poly-morphous-perverse) libidinal economy released from the dominion of a 'transcendental signified', itself equated with the bygone regime of capitalist and patriarchal power.[167]

Such was the *Tel Quel* brand of 'semiotic materialism', a grafting of linguistic (Saussurean) onto Marxist (Althusserian) and psychoanalytic (Lacanian) categories. Thus writing – *écriture* in the strong (post-structuralist) or qualitative sense of that term – could now be construed as a struggle to liberate the text's plural signifiers as against the 'surplus value' extracted by conventional reading practices whose fixation on the signified supposedly aligned them with the bourgeois drive to negate all forms of signifying excess, all challenges to the order of discourse (or of subject-positions in language) imposed by a false and oppressive reality-principle.[168] Needless to say this was a fragile, fissile conjuncture of ideas which soon fell apart under the mounting strain of post-1968 disenchantment on the French intellectual left. Hence no doubt the very sharp divergencies of theoretical and political allegiance that marked the break-up of the *Tel Quel* collective. In fact they ranged from various forms of revisionist Marxism to the weird brew of Catholic mysticism and Solzhenytsin-inspired Cold War polemics that marked the ascendance to media fame of the conservative *Nouveaux Philosophes*.[169]

Kristeva, I should emphasize, was never a party to this kind of wholesale reactive retreat. Her later work – from the mid-1970s on – was largely concerned with issues in language, feminism, and psychoanalysis. It continued to draw upon Lacanian concepts (the Mirror Stage, the Imaginary, the Symbolic, the Real), along with such categories as the abject, melancholia, and – most crucially – the *semiotic* as that realm of pre-Symbolic, pre-Oedipal drives and instinctual rhythmic energies that enabled certain writers to transgress or disrupt the protocols of bivalent logic, linear narrative, and realist representation.[170] These writers occupied the subject-position of 'woman' in the sense that their texts ran athwart the typically male ('phallogocentric') discourses of knowledge and truth. Moreover they enjoyed a privileged access to the semiotic realm, vouchsafed through their continuing (if intermittent) communion with the maternal *chora*, or by their not having passed – like the 'normal' male child in Freudian theory – through the enforced break with that sustaining element entailed by his 'successful' negotiation of the Oedipal crisis. All the same there were a few male writers – a rather motley company including Sade, Lautréamont, Mallarmé,

Céline, and Joyce – whose practice of a radically transgressive style enabled them to achieve what was, in efffect, a surrogate form of *écriture féminine.*[171] That is to say, such writing exhibited a whole range of markedly 'deviant' features – polysemy, metalepsis, disjunct narrative sequences, temporal elisions, compulsive rhythmic patterns, semantic overdetermination, discrepancies between manifest and latent meaning, dislocations of logico-semantic structure etc. – all of which bore witness to the semiotic and its power to disrupt the symbolic regime through the agency of repressed (polymorphous-perverse) desire.

It might appear something of a problem for Kristeva's theory that her claim for these writers as vanguard figures in the 'revolution of poetic language' is so completely at odds with what is known of their political and sexual orientation from other (presumably reliable) sources. Even discounting Sade – whose 'radical' status among French intellectuals makes him a special-case anomaly – one is left with a singularly hybrid group whose attitudes range from Olympian detachment, through Joyce's (to say the least) quirkish blend of socialism and feminism, to the extreme case (Céline) of a writer notorious for his antisemitic, violently misogynist and proto-fascist views. The fact that they are all male authors seems, by comparison, a minor difficulty. Of course this rendition is far from doing justice to a large and sophisticated body of work. My point is rather that these writings of Kristeva bring together all the themes – difference, textuality, radical otherness, truth and knowledge as discursive constructs, the subject as likewise an effect of language, a point of intersection between the Real, the Imaginary, and the Symbolic – which have pretty much dictated the agenda of radical French theory over the past two decades and more. And this remained the case when Kristeva gave up the *Marxisant* rhetoric of that early 'semioclastic' phase – the language of semiotic materialism and signifying practice – and devoted herself more to issues in the realm of feminism, ethics, and psychoanalysis. For she still subscribed to the two main articles of textualist thought: first, that questions of truth and subjectivity were accessible only through pre-given structures of linguistic representation, and second, that any 'radical' approach to these questions could be achieved only by treating the 'other' – the schizoid, psychotic, or marginalized other – as the locus of an absolute alterity beyond all the normative structures of rational sense-making discourse. Like Foucault in *Madness and Civilization* she identified otherness as the sole point of resistance to instituted discourses of power/knowledge. Which is also to say that she confused *normativity* – the condition of all intelligible thought and language – with the *normalizing* drive to supppress such otherness in the name of some ultimate (logocentric or patriarchal) truth.

It is therefore understandable that her latest books should have occasioned some surprise – and some rapid reappraisals – among Kristeva's followers in the post-structuralist camp. For they bring out very clearly the distance that she has moved from the entire set of counter-enlightenment theses – or the position on matters of language, subjectivity, and cultural otherness – outlined above. Indeed one might conjecture that Kristeva has travelled much the same route (and for some of the same reasons) that emerged in the case of Said. Both books are concerned with the eminently Kantian question: how far can we be justified in supposing that there exists a community of interests (cognitive, ethical, and socio-political) beyond the manifest fact of linguistic and cultural difference? And again: how can 'we' (on our own terms) 'enlightened' and 'progressive' secular intellectuals presume to speak on behalf of that wider community without laying claim to a universal wisdom that suppresses difference and thus writes another chapter in the violent history of Western ethnocentrism?

Such questions would of course receive a short answer from anyone convinced by the postmodern–textualist argument that equates all talk of reason and truth with the discourse of cultural imperialism. To Kristeva's previous way of thinking they would similarly be viewed as mere rationalizations of a Symbolic Order which extends its sway over all subjects – colonizers and colonized alike – by maintaining the authority of the paternal *logos* and suppressing the otherwise anarchic potential of the unbound semiotic drives. In Lyotard also (and I am thinking here of an early work like *Economie Libidinale*) one finds this connection between a vaguely conceived liberatory politics and an appeal to the Freudian 'polymorphous-perverse' as that realm of pre-symbolic impulses and desires that can somehow break through the oppressive structures of socialized discourse and rationality.[172] In both cases – Kristeva and Lyotard – it joins up readily enough with a theory of linguistic difference (or of multiple and heterogeneous 'phrase-regimes') which identifies subject-centred reason as the source of all oppression and injustice, and which invokes some notion of otherness, or absolute alterity, as the sole effective locus of resistance. On this highly selective reading of Freud such otherness has its seat in the libidinal economy – the rich and chaotic pre-Oedipal phase – that constitutes the realm of infantile sexuality. The result – as Terry Eagleton has recently remarked – is a constant two-way drift or slide between the high theoreticist discourse of 'classic' post-structuralism and a quasi-somatic, bodily, or sexualized register that reduces the subject to a passive arena of conflicting impulses and drives.[173]

'Let him still mark us, he shall see / Small change, when we're to bodies gone,' Donne's lines (from 'The Ecstasie') could aptly be taken as an ironic commentary on much of this recent theorizing. For it has, to say the least, some very dubious implications when extended to the spheres of ethics, politics, or cultural and gender difference. This debate has been engaged most actively by feminists who reject the idea – not only 'essentialist' but reductive, demeaning, and implicitly patriarchal – of 'woman' as a subject-position defined by its proximity to those pre-symbolic modes of *jouissance*, irrationality, polymorphous-perverse pleasure, and so forth.[174] For this is merely to invert (not contest or deconstruct) the traditional order of prejudice. It is a move that claims to give 'woman' pride of place while in fact reproducing all those value-laden binary terms (male/ female, reason/unreason, mind/body, intellect/instinct) that have hitherto contributed to the oppression of women. And there is another point here that has not been lost upon women critical of the 'men in feminism' movement, that is to say, the suspiciously convenient idea that since gender-positions are 'constructed in language', therefore it is open to the good-willed (reconstructed) male to adopt a feminist posture simply by 'reading as a woman', or electing to occupy the woman's position *vis-à-vis* the discourse of patriarchal truth and reason.[175] For such arguments have something of a boomerang effect, a double-edged tendency to celebrate (or exploit) the erotic possibilities of a feminized image-repertoire from a standpoint – that of 'theory' – which assumes all the typecast masculine prerogatives. And this applies even (or especially) to a text of extreme self-reflexive subtlety like Derrida's *Spurs*, his presentation of Nietzsche – most overtly misogynist of male thinkers – as a crypto-feminist whose writing evokes woman as the privileged 'nontruth' of philosophy, a name for whatever beguiles, seduces, provokes, or disconcerts the discourse of male reason.[176] For here again the question arises: to whom does all this pleasure accrue, the pleasure (that is) of treating 'woman' as philosophy's other, she whose erotic play of appearances – whose endless 'feigning', whether of truth-effects or of multiple simulated orgasm – supposedly offers a standing rebuke to the earnest male seeker-after-truth, but in fact (one suspects) rather more in the way of hypercultivated masculine sexual/textual arousal. Perhaps we had better read *Spurs* as a *reductio ad absurdum* of the 'otherness' argument, a cautionary instance of the way that this topos – along with its associated range of textualist strategies – can be turned back against even the most adept practitioner.

That this is also the case with 'otherness' construed in ethnic, cultural, or linguistic terms has been the chief burden of my argument in this book. Hence what I signalled (rather sketchily) above as the importance of Kristeva's re-thinking of these questions in *Strangers to Ourselves* and *Nations Without Nationalism*. For if there is one major theme that unites these books – and which sets them at odds with the received post-structuralist wisdom – it is their argument that we must find ways of interpreting 'otherness' which avoid the twin dangers of rhetorical vacuity and paranoid reactive definition. Most important here is Kristeva's marked change of attitude with regard to the role of Enlightenment ('cosmopolitan') thinking as a crucial phase in the coming-to-terms with issues of cultural alterity and difference. Like Derrida, she sees that any genuinely other-regarding ethics or politics must always be prepared to recognize the other as in some sense an *alter ego*, a subject – or person – whose being could exert no claim upon one's moral conscience if thought of as somehow existing in a realm of absolute, intransigent otherness. For this latter way of thinking provides no defence against the vicious downward spiral – the projection of difference in negative (racial or ethnic) terms – which the discourse of nationalism can readily exploit. Such resistance comes only from the kind of self-knowledge that discovers alterity within itself, that is to say, as a certain unknowability that inhabits even our most familiar thoughts and actions. This is what makes us 'strangers to ourselves', reflective agents whose destiny it is both to seek enlightenment (lucid understanding and access to the universal 'kingdom of ends') as an ultimate good, and at the same time always to acknowledge the limits placed upon any such enterprise. It is also, according to Kristeva, the source of much that is best in the tradition of Western philosophic and ethical thought. For if thinking is caught up in this inward dialectic of self and other then it will have more reason – by analogy with its own experience – to extend such tolerance toward those who exist (or come in from) outside its cultural domain.

Again I can offer only a brief summary of these two densely argued and powerfully evocative texts. In *Strangers to Ourselves* Kristeva's main purpose is to highlight those episodes in the Western intellectual and literary tradition where the encounter takes place between a reason willing to question its own certitudes and an 'otherness' perceived not as *radically* other but as likewise set about by all the problems and perplexities that characterize human understanding. At such moments there occurs what Paul de Man describes – in a different but not unrelated context – as the alternating rhythm of 'blindness' and 'insight', or of knowledge arrived at through a process of self-chastening reflection on that which eludes its own best powers of conscious theoretical grasp. Indeed I would instance 'Crisis and Criticism', de Man's early essay on Husserl, as a paradigm case of the way that these antinomies can press into regions of the ethical 'unconscious' – its latent complexities of meaning and motive – beyond any straightforward appeal to the author's (Husserl's or indeed de Man's) knowing intent.[177] Husserl, we may recall, had written of the 'crisis' of European philosophy as if that crisis were of world-historical proportions and thereby justified his treating other cultures as – in de Man's words – 'primitive, pre-scientific and pre-philosophical, myth-dominated and congenitally incapable of the disinterested distance without which there can be no philosophical meditation'.[178] And this despite the fact that, *on his own account*, philosophy aspired to the status of a universal discourse transcending all such merely localized, contingent, or culture-specific boundaries. Thus Husserl's project 'necessarily tends toward a universality that finds its concrete, geographical correlative in the formation of supratribal, supernational communities such as, for instance, Europe'.[179] But of course this begs the question – duly noted by de Man – as to '(w)hy this geographical expansion should have chosen to stop, once and forever, at the Atlantic Ocean and the Caucasus'.[180]

What is at issue here is neither Husserl's moral character (as undoubtedly 'a man of superior goodwill') nor yet his commitment to an enterprise – that of transcendental phenomenology – whose value and whose 'rigorous' necessity de Man is at pains to acknowledge. Rather, it is a matter of applying to Husserl precisely those

standards – of goodwill, rigour, and critical acumen – which characterize that project at its best. For it then becomes clear, in de Man's
words, that 'the crucial, determining examination on which depends
Husserl's right to call himself, by his own terms, a philosopher, is in
fact never undertaken'.[181] And again: '[a]s a European, it seems that
Husserl escapes from the necessary self-criticism that is prior to all
philosophical truth about the self'.[182] Thus the point is not at all that
Husserl's project must be viewed as in some way naive, misconceived, or radically flawed. Nor is it to argue – in postmodern
fashion – that Husserl is just the last, most 'radical' exponent of an
outworn critical–enlightenment tradition whose bankruptcy he
demonstrates all the more tellingly by pushing its premises to their
self-defeating limit. On the contrary: it is only by reading Husserl
with the benefit of his own best insights that we can understand those
ingrained forces of prejudice and assumptions of cultural superiority
that conspired to prevent his project from attaining the kind of
universal validity it sought. His text thus becomes an object-lesson in
the complex dialectic of 'blindness' and 'insight' that de Man finds
typical of all such statements in the 'crisis-determined' mode. That is
to say, '[i]t establishes an important truth: the fact that philosophical
knowledge can only come into being when it is turned back upon
itself'. But at the same time – and (as de Man argues) by an order of
structural necessity – it 'proceeds . . . to do just the opposite . . . The
rhetoric of crisis states its own truth in the mode of error. It is itself
radically blind to the light it emits'.[183]

Still we should be wrong to conclude from all this that enlightenment critique henceforth stands revealed as a delusive or bad-faith
enterprise, one whose professions of emancipatory intent are everywhere bound up with a domineering drive to subjugate cultural
difference and otherness. For in the end, as de Man well knows, we
have no choice but to keep faith with Husserl's conception of philosophy as 'a process by means of which naive assumptions are made
accessible to consciousness by an act of critical self-understanding',
or again as 'a persistently reflective attitude that can take philosophy
itself for its theme'.[184] And this despite the inherent danger – the risk
of ethnocentrism, arrogance, or worse – which attends any project
like Husserl's, that is, any thinking that brackets or suspends the
natural (pre-reflective) attitude. Such thought is always prone to
delusions of epistemological and ethical grandeur, to rehearsing a
displaced scene of colonial encounter, or 'what takes place when the

superior theoretical man observes the inferior natural man'. But it is
equally the case that we can perceive such lapses – such blind-spots
of prejudice and motivating interest – only through a better, more
enlightened and self-critical exercise of reason. What de Man charac-
teristically asserts in negative form (that there is no critical 'insight'
without some accompanying moment of necessary 'blindness') can
also be read, so to speak, in reverse, as yielding the surely more
hopeful lesson that insight may indeed come about by reflection on
those same deeply-ingrained sources of error and partisan judgment.
And it is here that Kristeva's recent work provides a counterpart – a
qualified affirmative view – to set against de Man's dark-hued
meditations. For it offers a defence of those regulative ideas (progress, democracy, freedom, cosmopolitanism, the universalist conception of human rights) which have always – at least since the
ancient Greeks – held out an alternative to the dominant forms of
self-defined ethnic and national identity. And it does so, moreover,
through a reading of the relevant texts and historical evidence which
amounts to the strongest of arguments against any premature retreat
into 'postmodern' postures of indifference, cynicism, or despair.

Of course I am not suggesting (absurdly) that Kristeva has undergone some kind of wholesale dramatic conversion to the principles
and values of Enlightenment thought. Indeed her books contain
many passages of sobering reflection on the persistence of nationalist
sentiment in its more atavistic or paranoid forms, on the constant
possibility of vicious downward spirals in the relation between
cultural identity and otherness, and on the forces of unreason,
bigotry, and hatred ranged against the hope for peaceful coexistence.
Certainly she yields nothing to de Man when it comes to
acknowledging the resistance that enlightenment confronts, not least
the internal resistance put up by its own more settled, complacent, or
dogmatic habits of thought. And in her case – unlike de Man's – the
consequences are worked out with reference to particular real-world
conflicts and specific (often violent) enactments of cultural difference
which permit of no escape to that alternative realm where everything
becomes (in the last instance) a textualized 'allegory of reading'. So
one could not accuse Kristeva of merely looking on the bright side or
adopting some abstract-utopian view at oods with the melancholy
witness of historical events.

Let me cite the first paragraph of *Strangers to Ourselves* since it
presents both arguments – 'negative' and 'positive' – with a

maximum sense of their resistance to any kind of facile (quasi-Hegelian) overcoming.

> Foreigner: a choked up rage deep within my throat, a black angel clouding transparency, an opaque, unfathomable spur. The image of hatred and of the other, a foreigner is neither the romantic victim of our clannish indolence nor the intruder responsible for all the ills of the polis . . . Strangely, the foreigner lives within us: he is the hidden face of our identity, the space that wrecks our abode, the time in which understanding and affinity founder. By recognizing him within ourselves, we are spared detesting him in himself. A symptom that precisely turns 'we' into a problem, perhaps makes it impossible. The foreigner comes in when the consciousness of my difference arises, and he disappears when we all acknowledge ourselves as foreigners, unamenable to bonds and communities.[185]

From 'choked up rage', via 'clannish indolence', to the acknowledgment of difference, strangeness, or alterity as that which also exists *within ourselves*, and hence as a solvent of ethnic or racial animosity – such is Kristeva's argument here and in numerous subsequent passages of her book. As I have said, it is an argument that takes full stock of the recalcitrant evidence – the historical setbacks, periods of resurgent nationalist strife, violence against immigrant communities, outbreaks of xenophobic hatred, and so forth – which are grist to the mill of postmodernist or counter-enlightenment commentators. There is always the danger of such regressive (paranoid) projections of cultural otherness, especially – as at present – in times of widespread socio-political upheaval when national boundaries (and ego-boundaries) are perceived as under threat. Nevertheless, '[w]hen we flee from or struggle against the foreigner, we are fighting our unconscious – that "improper" facet of our impossible "own and proper" '.[186] For if there is one lesson that Freud should have taught us – and which makes the findings of psychoanalysis central to her argument in this book – it is the fact that we are indeed 'strangers to ourselves' in a sense that paradoxically points a way beyond the violent confrontation of self and other. 'The foreigner is within me, hence we are all foreigners.'

For Kristeva this perception has large consequences, not least as regards our understanding of 'enlightenment' in both its period-specific usage and as a wider phenomenon in the history of Western (post-Hellenic) thought. What it signifies chiefly is the non-contradiction – the absence of any necessary conflict – between the good-willed attempt to comprehend others on the basis of certain, if not 'universal' then at any rate widely held (and reasonably inferred) beliefs, values, knowledge-constitutive interests etc., and the due recognition of cultural otherness as a part of that entitlement that we ourselves share in relation to the element of strangeness (Freud's 'unncanny') to which our own experience bears witness. Montaigne is one of her great exemplars here, for reasons that I have hinted at above with reference to the growth of 'Renaissance scepticism' and its marked (if gradual) civilizing influence on Christian doctrine and practices. Thus Kristeva cites Montaigne on 'that other life of mine that lies in the knowledge of my friends', on the puzzles and antinomies of selfhood ('but we are, I know not how, double within ourselves'), and on the sheer multiplicity of so-called 'human nature' ('there is more distance from a given man to a given man than from a given man to a given animal').[187] To this extent at least Montaigne is in agreement with those postmodern celebrants of the decentred, the fragmented or discontinuous 'self' that requires no 'deep further fact' of personal identity – no unified subject or Kantian 'transcendental unity of apperception' – through which to make sense of its fleeting memories, impressions, and desires. 'We are all patchwork, and so shapeless and diverse in composition that each bit, each moment, plays its own game. And there is as much difference between us and ourselves as between us and others.'[188] Oddly enough Kristeva makes no mention of Hume, despite the very similar linkage in his thought between a scepticism concerning the 'deep further fact', a lively curiosity as to the range of human life-forms, and a thoroughly naturalized (more atheist than agnostic) approach to the varieties of religious belief.[189] For these are exactly the qualities she values in Montaigne: his readiness to see all around a question by refusing any form of coercive doctrinal adherence.

But there is more to this attitude than appears if one takes Montaigne as an easygoing sceptic in the postmodern-pragmatist mould, or as adopting – like the New Historicists – the notion that 'truth' is nothing more than a product of localized power/knowledge interests. The difference emerges most plainly in his moral revulsion when confronted with the violence, hypocrisy and pious self-deception manifest in the treatment of 'barbarous' native populations by the emisssaries of 'civilized' European culture. His essay 'On Cannibals' is probably the best-known instance of how Montaigne contrives to turn such prejudices back against themselves and reveal the iniquities routinely practised in their name.[190] To this extent his writing may be said to prefigure that modern 'hermeneutics of suspicion' which informs the New Historicist idea of colonial discourse as a range of strategies – negotiative ruses – whose primary object is to contain, defuse or somehow domesticate the threat of cultural otherness.

Thus viewed, the encounter between colonizer and colonized becomes an allegory of 'difference' in general, a scene whose conflictual dynamics are best understood by analogy with language, textuality, representation, or what goes on in the endless struggle for interpretative mastery and power. But as Kristeva makes clear, such a reading can do scant justice to the *ethical* force of Montaigne's reflection on the evils of colonial rule. Nor can it account convincingly for his outrage at events nearer home, like the forcible conversion of the Portuguese Jews under Spanish Catholic rule. What drops out of sight in New Historicism – as with other variations on the 'textual politics' theme – is the very idea that a thinker like Montaigne could move from a *knowledge* of contemporary events to a *reflective moral judgment* on those same events that put him decisively at odds with the dominant habits of belief in his time. Thus the 'presentist' bias of New Historicism – its inclination (following Foucault) to interpret everything from the viewpoint of a 'history of the present' – goes along with its very marked strain of political quietism or *Kulturpessimismus*. Both attitudes derive from a kind of methodological solipsism, a root conviction that nothing can be known (or be subject to any kind of reasoning judgment) aside from the discourses that currently comprise what shall count as admissible belief.

This attitude stands in marked contrast to Kristeva's reading of Montaigne. Here also there is a stress on the self-reflexive quality of his writing, its sceptical bias and its willingness to question every last certitude of 'civilized' thought. Moreover, this scepticism clearly extended to that idea of autonomous selfhood – of the subject as a locus of self-identical knowledge, experience, and judgment – whose selective application Montaigne perceived as a harmful illusion and a source of much injustice. But these abuses came about through the kind of reflex ethnocentric thinking that viewed rationality as strictly the prerogative of European man, and which took it for granted that other cultures had not yet attained – or were incapable of attaining – any such privileged standpoint. This is what distinguishes Montaigne's scepticism from the wholesale varieties currently in vogue among postmodernists, New Historicists, and others. It works on a principle directly counter to the 'radical alterity' thesis: that is to say, on the assumption that however deep such cultural differences may run, they are still (in William Empson's fine phrase) 'a small thing by comparison with our common humanity'.[191] The trouble with the current anti-humanist *doxa* is that it swings so far against those bad old forms of quasi-universalist subject-centred thought that it leaves no room for treating other subjects – including the victims of colonial oppression – as in any way capable of reasoned enquiry or reflective moral awareness. At this point scepticism passes over into cynicism, or the critique of prejudice into another (just as damaging) kind of prejudice that regards all truth-claims and ethical values as relative to this or that 'discourse', or again, as mere products of the will-to-power in its protean manifestations.

Hence the inability of critics like Greenblatt to conceive that there might be something more to 'Renaissance scepticism' than a merely reactive attitudinal shift or the exchange of one subject-position for another within the limits laid down by some existing discursive economy. Again it is worth recalling what de Man has to say about the prejudicial blind-spots that emerge through a symptomatic reading of Husserl's text on transcendental phenomenology and the 'crisis' of the European sciences. His point is not that we should abandon the heritage of Enlightenment critique on account of its failure (in Husserl and others) to live up to its own highest standards of moral and intellectual conscience. Still less is it to urge, like Foucault, that we should renounce all thought of the subject – the knowing, judging, reflective, self-critical subject – except as a species of transcendental illusion, a figment of the humanist imaginary destined to imminent (and welcome) eclipse. On the contrary: it is only by respecting such claims *in ourselves and others* that we can hope to make progress beyond those forms of partiality, prejudice, and cultural arrogance that can be shown to have affected the judgment even of a thinker like Husserl, one whose intellectual acuity and 'superior goodwill' de Man never places in doubt.

Let me quote one further passage from Kristeva on Montaigne since it presents this case for enlightened understanding – and for what might be called a form of qualified universalism – with particular lucidity and force. 'Whether or not they could have had the spirit of Montaigne or been able to take advantage of his writings, I imagine the great travellers, ethnologists, and explorers of the

Renaissance developed in like manner.'[192] And this conjecture is justified, she goes on to argue, by exactly those qualities in Montaigne's writing – self-reflexive, sceptical, supremely undogmatic, willing to generalize but only on the basis of perceived common failings and shared liabilities – which hold out against any kind of orthodox doctrinal imposition.

> One must indeed first be securely grounded in oneself, be cognizant of one's wretchedness and one's glory, be able to talk about them in a straightforward manner – without banality or pathos. Then, the self that has thus been created, rather than such and such a land, religion, court, or policy will become the port of departure for that other Renaissance, which, beyond the nations that are taking shape, draws comparisons, makes relative, renders universal. A new cosmopolitanism is being born, no longer founded on the unity of creatures belonging to God, as Dante conceived, but on the universality of a self that is fragile, casual, and nevertheless virtuous and certain. Montaigne's self, which never ceases to travel in the self, is already an invitation to explore the world and others with the same uncompromising kindness.[193]

This passage would bear a great deal of commentary, not least by way of contrastive analysis when set against some of Kristeva's earlier theoretical positions. Clearly she has shifted ground on a number of issues, among them the idea of subjectivity as a textual or discursive construct, the equation between radical politics and forms of 'transgressive' (polymorphous-perverse) desire, and the kindred supposition that 'reason' and 'truth' are mere ruses in the service of a normalizing discourse aimed at suppressing such disruptive effects. For the passage has a wider (indeed a normative) bearing on the whole line of argument developed in *Strangers to Ourselves*. Most importantly, it centres on that complex of themes – self and other, identity and difference, the claims of universalist ('enlightenment') reason *vis-à-vis* the claims of linguistic, cultural, or ethnic alterity – which post-structuralism treats as binary terms in a strictly non-negotiable, antagonist relation. And from here, as I have argued, it is no great distance to the hideous rhetoric of 'ethnic cleansing' and the various strains of revived nationalist fervour that also ride high on the current wave of reactive counter-enlightenment thought.

This entire way of thinking is thrown into question by Kristeva's commentary on Montaigne. To be 'securely grounded in oneself' is *not* – or not necessarily – to impose one's culture-specific values and

beliefs on those beyond the 'civilized' pale. Nor is it a matter (as the
New Historicists and neo-pragmatists would argue) of our having no
choice – like Montaigne and his contemporaries – but to go along
with the languages, the discourses or cultural mores that define the
limits of permissible thinking at any given time. For this whole
debate has been skewed – so Kristeva implies – in such a way as to
make these appear the only alternatives. What is thereby concealed
from view is the hopeful possibility that Montaigne holds out,
namely that of the 'other Renaissance' (or the 'new cosmopolitanism') that in Kristeva's carefully chosen words 'draws
comparisons, makes relative, renders universal'. Her conjoining this
latter pair of phrases will seem a flat contradiction in terms only if
one takes it as read – in postmodernist fashion – that *any* appeal to
'universal' values must *ipso facto* involve a refusal to acknowledge
the diversity of human beliefs. But there is nothing oxymoronic'
about Kristeva's phrasing here, any more than in her reference to
'uncompromising kindness', or again, to 'the universality of a self
that is fragile, casual, and nevertheless virtuous and certain'. Of
course it may be asked how these two lines of talk can possibly be
squared; how Kristeva can find 'universal' significance in Montaigne's restless scepticism, his questioning of all taken-for-granted
truth-claims and values. And what shall we make of this self whose
purported 'universality' comes of its existing in a state at once
'fragile' (as post-structuralists would readily agree) and at the same
time somehow 'virtuous and certain'? It does seem that Kristeva's
formulations are designed to provoke maximum resistance both
among adherents to the 'enlightenment' line on autonomy, reason,
and truth and among those who would summarily reject that line in
the name of difference, alterity, and cultural relativism.

But this reading is itself symptomatic of the self-imposed dilemma
– the false polarization of attitudes – that has bedevilled so much
recent discussion of these issues. That Kristeva now talks about the
'self' rather than the 'subject' is one clear sign that she wishes to
break with the kind of theoretical deadlock that post-structuralism
created (and which her own early work did much to encourage) by
dissolving subjectivity into the structures of language, discourse, or
representation. For without some stronger, more substantive notion
of the self there can be no accounting for ethical agency, for the
powers of reflective, self-critical thought, or whatever it was that
enabled a thinker like Montaigne to question the received self-

images of his age.[194] This is why post-structuralism and its New Historicist offshoot are so utterly lacking in conceptual and ethical resoures when it comes to explaining how changes have occurred – fitfully, no doubt, but often with momentous consequences – in the spheres of human moral and political awareness. All that they can offer is a textualist (discourse-theoretical) variant on the old empiricist notion of the subject as a *tabula rasa*, a passive receptacle for whatever impressions, ideas, or meanings happen to constitute the current range of ideological structures-in-dominance. Any resistance to those structures can only be attributed to a reflex tendency for power to generate some counter-discourse likewise complicit with the omnipresent workings of power/knowledge.

That this process is thought of as *reflexive* rather than *reflective* – that is to say, as reducing the self to an empty locus (or 'subject-position') traversed by these conflicting lines of force – is one measure of the poverty of post-structuralist theory. Another is its having no option but to interpret a free-thinking sceptic like Montaigne – or (in Greenblatt's case) the generalized 'discourse' of Renaissance scepticism – as likewise just an instance of the cultural dynamic that constitutes subjects in the force-field of linguistic difference. For what is thus ruled out, as a species of naive 'transcendental' illusion, is the very idea that moral and political progress may sometimes come about through *conscious reflection* on the link between knowledge and power, and through a clear-eyed perception of the interests at stake in preventing such an exercise of critical thought.

To this extent New Historicism falls in with the kind of cynical *Realpolitik* – much in evidence among right-wing ideologues, past and present – which denies that reason or 'enlightened' thought have any role to play in the course of history, in the shaping of political institutions, or in working towards a more just and equitable social order. Indeed there is a close resemblance between talk of 'market forces' as an all-purpose regulative mechanism, one that permits of no state 'interference' on ethical or policy grounds, and that strain of quasi-radical thought which likewise sees nothing but error and delusion in the 'discourse' of emancipatory critique. Thus in both cases there is a strong deflationary drive with regard to the values of reason, justice, and truth; to the subject's role as thinker and potential agent of change; and to the normative claims of any ethics (or politics) beyond what is dictated by the so-called 'laws' of the market, or by the play of differential forces within some existing discursive regime. Nor is this comparison rendered absurd by the disparity between their overt political agendas. For if 'radicalism' is by no means an exclusive prerogative of the left – as we have learnt all too painfully in recent years – then it is also the case that left-sounding radicalism of, for instance, the post-structuralist or New Historicist variety may turn out to harbour some decidedly conservative implications.

IX

Persons, not subjects: community and difference

I have emphasized the 'enlightenment' aspects of Kristeva's recent writing since they mark both a new direction in her work and a useful means of address to these larger ethical, social, and political issues. Of course my account is open to the criticism that it offers a highly selective reading, one that ignores her countervailing stress on that element of the 'foreign', the 'strange' or 'uncanny' in the absence of which enlightenment can indeed become a discourse of monological (or instrumental) reason mirrored in the history of colonial oppression. I should therefore acknowledge that her book contains many passages – among them some of its most eloquent and powerful – that could well be cited in support of a reading markedly at odds with my own. Certainly she is far from ignoring the danger – the potential for spiralling hatred and paranoid suspicion – that goes along with this at-best uneasy dialectic of cultural identity and otherness. It is the theme of her chapter on Camus's *L'Etranger*, which she reads as a bleak but in many ways pinpoint diagnosis of the psychopathology of ultimate inward and outward alienation. Thus Meursault 'carries to an extreme the separateness of the uprooted person: his walled-in violence against others . . . a fragmentation bomb, the calm, icy distrust of the protagonists for one another creating the only link within this conglomerate of condemned people'.[195] But it is also – less dramatically – a constant burden of her thoughts about the history of encounters with 'foreignness', from the ancient Greeks and the Graeco-Roman Stoics to Freud's late writings (very much in the stoical tradition) on civilization and its discontents. Thus in Freud '(t)he violent, catastrophic aspect the encounter with the *foreigner* may assume is to be included in the generalizing consequences that seem to stem out of (his) observations on the activating of the uncanny'.[196] And the tone of those writings – dark-hued and sombre – is certainly not such as to encourage any facile hopes for deliverance out of all our present-day afflictions.

But to stress only these dire intimations in Kristeva's book would be just as one-sided as a reading that screened them out and focused solely on the gleams of Enlightenment faith. What occurs most often – sometimes in the space of a single sentence – is that Kristeva moves on from acknowledging the worst possibilities (difference as a cause of hatred, paranoia, ethnic persecution) to the prospect of a better, more enlightened alternative where the difference *within* each and every subject is envisaged as providing the common ground, the measure of shared humanity, whereby to transcend such differences *between* ethnic and national ties. Thus: '(b)eing aware of that infernal dynamics of estrangement at the heart of each entity, individual, or group certainly distances one from eighteenth-century optimism but *without calling the principle into question*' (my italics).[197] It is in this spirit that Kristeva appeals to those Enlightenment (or proto-Enlightenment) thinkers – Erasmus, Thomas More, Montaigne, Montesquieu, Diderot, Kant, Thomas Paine – who in various ways tried to reconcile the claims of a respect for the diversity of human cultures and a commitment to the 'cosmopolitan' ideals of universal justice and truth. Her point, once again, is that these values are not incompatible so long as one avoids the (nowadays prevalent) mistake of equating 'Enlightenment' with a body of *doctrine* whose universality can be maintained only by ignoring its origins in a certain (culture-specific) time and place. For Kristeva – as indeed for liberal theorists like Rawls – this mistake is what has chiefly stood in the way of a genuine (democratic) universalism that *transcends without suppressing* the variety of human interests, values, political allegiances, and so forth.

Kristeva makes the point as follows in a passage that could easily be taken for Rawls in one of his recent essays on the topic of 'justice as fairness'. 'Now it is possible', she comments *à propos* the French *Declaration of the Rights of Man and Citizen*,

> to separate, in the spirit of eighteenth-century humanism, its *principle* from its *content*. While it is true that the content is wedded to the abstract notion of human nature, reduced in a now outdated manner to 'liberty', 'property', and 'sovereignty', the principle does remain, and it has a twofold bearing. On the one hand it inherits the stoic and Christian tradition of universality, and postulates its immanence here

and now in speaking subjects. On the other hand it has the pragmatic advantage of being centered in the reality of political institutions, without being limited to them. The idea is to postulate an ethical value without confusing it with historical society and its vagaries.[198]

My comparison with Rawls may appear far-fetched, given Kristeva's very different disciplinary background and intellectual formation. But it is helpful partly as a clarifying gloss from that 'other' (Anglo-American) tradition and partly by virtue of her own changed attitude with regard to these issues. There are three main points that I wish to take up from Rawls's recent writings, among them his Dewey lectures ('Kantian Constructivism in Moral Theory') and his 1985 essay 'Justice as Fairness: political not metaphysical'.[199] The first has to do with his concept of the *person* as a bearer of interests, rights, and obligations that belong to him or her as a 'representative' citizen, and that should – ideally – be treated as distinct from their particular status (advantaged or otherwise) in some given social order. This is of course the argument propounded in Rawls's book *A Theory of Justice*.[200] There it takes the form of a thought-experiment where persons are imagined as deliberating on questions of equality, freedom, distributive justice etc. from an 'original position' (or from behind a 'veil of ignorance') which allows them to discount for personal motives and preferences.

Rawls's second point – connected with this – is that 'persons' thus conceived have interests and rights which need not involve any ultimate ('metaphysical') appeal to some essence of humanity or universal ground of reason, knowledge, or value. Thus the concept of the person, according to Rawls, 'must be distinguished from specifications of the concept of the self as knower, used in epistemology or metaphysics, or the concept of the self as the continuant carrier of psychological states: the self as substance, or soul'.[201] Rather, we should think of the person as 'a human being capable of taking full part in social cooperation, honoring its ties and relationships over a full life'.[202] And this latter conception must necessarily find room for a wide range of possible views with regard to the relevant values and priorities. For these views will vary depending, for instance, 'on how social cooperation or a complete life is conceived; and each such specification yields another conception of the person falling under the concept'.[203] This leads on to Rawls's third main point, in reply to those critics – among them liberal-communitarians like Michael Walzer – who reject what they see as his exccessively 'formalist' approach.[204] That is to say, one cannot derive any genuine (substantive) principles of justice from a rational-choice theory that reduces the 'person' to an artefact of its own abstract contriving, and which takes no account of the social context – or cultural life-world – wherein such choices acquire meaning and significance. Rawls answers this criticism by distinguishing between 'reasonableness' and 'rationality', the first having to do with those social virtues (primarily the commitment to freedom and equality) that define a liberal polity, and the second with the various strategic choices that individuals may pursue out of perceived self-interest but also in conformity with those primary goods. Thus '[i]n justice as fairness, the Reasonable frames the Rational and is derived from a conception of moral persons as free and equal'.[205] From which it follows that 'the principles of justice and the rights and liberties they define cannot, in such a society, be overridden by considerations of efficiency and a greater net balance of social well-being'.[206] But the charge of formalism misses its mark in so far as these principles legislate only for issues of 'pure procedural justice at the highest level'. For as Rawls acknowledges there exist large differences in the way that individuals – and indeed political theorists – see fit to interpret or apply them as a matter of detailed recommendation. (Thus the Rawlsian argument would need to find room even for so markedly divergent a notion of 'liberalism' as that put forward by his conservative opponent Robert Nozick.)[207] There is nothing in his theory that precludes the idea of individuals exercising a large measure of freedom with regard to those particular choices that remain – and which give their lives a sense of meaning and purpose – in a working liberal democracy.

What sets Rawls apart from the communitarians – as likewise from neo-pragmatists like Rorty – is his belief that one can *both* make adequate allowance for this range of culture-specific interests, values, and priorities, *and* maintain the principled appeal to higher-level maxims of 'justice as fairness'. So it is with his concept of the person: a double-aspect theory that seeks to hold in balance the 'capacity for a sense of justice' (belonging to that higher-level public or citizenly realm) and the 'capacity for a conception of the good' (which may involve all manner of 'attachments to other persons and loyalties to various groups and associations'). These latter 'give rise to affections and devotions, and therefore the flourishing of the persons and associations who are the objects of these sentiments is also part of our conception of the good'. Moreover, any such conception must include 'a view of our relation to the world – religious, philosophical, or moral – by reference to which the value and significance of our ends are understood'.[208] But in Rawls's view (again *contra* the liberal-communitarians) there are still questions that arise as to the justice or fairness of those ends, quite apart from their playing a meaningful role in our own (or some other) cultural form of life. It is by achieving what he calls a 'reflective equillibrium' between these orders of judgment that we can best approximate the liberal ideal of an open and plural yet reasoned and principled mode of social existence. For one respect in which persons are regarded as free – or as autonomous moral agents in the Kantian sense – is that 'they are regarded as capable of taking responsibility for their ends', which in turn 'affects how their various claims are assessed'.

Thus the Rawlsian theory of justice entails, among other things, a higher valuation of individual freedom and responsibility than anything envisaged on those recent deflationary accounts – poststructuralist, postmodernist or neo-pragmatist – which typically treat the *subject* (rather than the person) as their prime candidate for whatever remains in the way of autonomous agency and choice. In its moderate (communitarian) guise this argument holds that we can best avoid the troublesome antinomies of formalist, i.e. Kantian, ethical theory by dropping all the needless talk of maxims or principles and deriving our various conceptions of the good from the currency of in-place values and beliefs.[209] Post-structuralism can be seen as a more 'radical' version of the same line of argument, starting out as it does – for polemical purposes – from a Cartesian idea of the self-transparent *cogito*, or 'subject-presumed-to-know', all the better to demolish that illusory notion and substitute its own preferential idiom of 'discourse', 'textuality', multiple and shifting 'subject-positions' etc.[210] And the way is then open for a postmodern–pragmatist–liberal–ironist like Rorty to declare himself frankly bored with that old (epistemological or subject-centred) paradigm, and to urge that we should henceforth regard such issues as a matter of simply taking one's choice between the various language-games (or 'final vocabularies') currently on offer. In effect what Rorty does is call the bluff of those thinkers on the poststructuralist left who think to derive some 'radical' politics from the wholesale dissolution – or 'decentring' – of the subject brought about by this linguistic turn. Thus he can treat even Foucault as a 'liberal ironist' concerned not so much with changing the world as with developing new metaphors, new possibilties of self-description which are (or which should be) wholly detached from issues in the public–political sphere.[211]

It is not hard to guess what Foucault might have said if confronted with this singular misreading of his life's work and record of activist dissident concern. But for Rorty such objections would carry no weight, first because he writes as a 'strong revisionist' to whom issues of truth (or interpretive fidelity) are in any case beside the point, and second because Foucault himself – in his Nietzsche-inspired sceptical genealogies of power/knowledge – invited such treatment by undermining the ground for any reasoned or principled response.[212] So one can see why Rawls holds it preferable to think about 'persons' (rather than 'subjects') as the basis for a workable theory of justice or an ethics capable of resisting the drift into forms of disabling value-relativism. Rorty's argument at least has the cautionary merit (or diagnostic virtue) of pushing all the way with this current trend and embracing the idea of a total split between the private and public realms. On the Rawlsian view, by contrast, the idea of personhood provides what is missing in all such drastically dichotomized accounts, namely a bridge – or a mediating concept – between individual and society. Thus persons can recognize 'that the weight of their claims is not given by the strength and psychological intensity of their wants and desires (as opposed to their needs and requirements as citizens), even when their wants and desires are rational from their point of view'.[213] And again: 'a political conception of the person articulates this idea and fits it into the idea of society as a system of social cooperation over a complete life'.[214] Nothing could more clearly indicate the political (as well as the moral) bankruptcy of postmodern thought than its casual assumption that any such ideas – betraying as they do an 'Enlightenment' pedigree – are nowadays hopelessly *dépassé*.

No doubt many readers will have thought it absurd (or a blatant piece of 'strong revisionism' on my part) to suggest Rawls as a relevant 'intertext' for understanding Kristeva's recent work. But if so then it is likely that they have read these books with certain fixed preconceptions carried over from acquaintance with her earlier (post-structuralist) thinking. Of course there is an alternative line of response for those still attached to that position but willing to concede the fact of Kristeva's having left it pretty much behind. That is to say, they might argue that this is just one more (albeit disheartening) instance of an erstwhile radical theorist coming around in mid-career to a far more conservative stance on issues of truth, knowledge, subjectivity, ethics, and politics. I think that exactly the opposite is the case and that Kristeva's change of theoretical heart is a response both to chronic liabilities in the post-structuralist paradigm and to real-world events which have brought that lesson home with uncomfortable force. For it is clear that she has those events very much in mind when she defends the universalist discourse of Enlightenment, the doctrine of human rights as set down in the classic texts of that tradition, and Montesquieu's appeal to '*l'esprit des lois*' as a regulative idea for the progress towards a truly 'cosmopolitan' ethico-political order.[215] Thus: '[i]t is only by maintaining the *principle* of that universal dignity – without scattering it among new national, religious, or private regionalisms – that one might consider modifying its *content*, taking into consideration what the behavior of human beings reveals as to their humanity'.[216] This 'modification' includes a large allowance for the facts of cultural difference, 'strangeness', and alterity, an allowance which – as Kristeva knows – was not always made by the avatars of Enlightenment in its more doctrinaire forms. But she is also convinced that any hope of redeeming those past errors and iniquities must rest with a better, more consistent and principled pursuit of Enlightenment ideals.

The issue, once again, is that taken up by Derrida in his essay on Levinas, and by de Man in his reflection on the kinds of prejudice – the blind-spots of ethnocentric thinking – that can inhabit even the texts of a scrupulous and 'good-willed' philosopher like Husserl. For there is no contesting such attitudes from the standpoint of a purely reactive (counter-enlightenment) ethos which makes a shibboleth of ethnic or cultural difference, and which denies all knowledge of the 'absolute other' except in the mode of a self-denying ordinance that owns itself utterly without resources in face of such radical alterity. Small wonder that Kristeva – like Said – has undergone a sharp conversion from this way of thinking when confronted with the testimony of recent events in Yugoslavia, Palestine, the ex-Soviet Republics, and elsewhere. What these events demonstrate with chilling regularity is the peril – the potential for human catastrophe – in the slide from an ethic of shared humanity across cultural

differences to a notion of 'otherness' that easily translates into forms
of rampant xenophobia. So it is that mixed communities of Serbs,
Croats, and Muslims can be one week living peaceably as neighbours
in the same village, and the next week conducting unspeakable
campaigns of 'ethnic cleansing', mass-murder, and systematic rape.
Indeed, this presents the most telling example of the way that seemingly 'abstract' issues are mirrored, enacted, or called to account by
turns of real-world historical event. If there is one such episode that
should give pause to the proponents of 'difference' and cultural
particularism it is the tragedy that has engulfed ex-Yugoslavia and
which also – as I write – threatens to attend the break-up of other
federalist states in Eastern Europe. And if there is one lesson to be
learned from all this it is the lesson that Kristeva so eloquently draws
in *Strangers to Ourselves* and *Nations Without Nationalism.*

Her position now amounts to a point-for-point rebuttal of the
entire post-structuralist *doxa* on Enlightenment and its supposed evil
legacy. 'The Nazis', she writes,

> did not lose their humanity because of the 'abstraction' that may have
> existed in the notion of 'man' . . . On the contrary – it is because they
> had lost the lofty, abstract, fully symbolic notion of humanity and
> replaced it with a local, national, or ideological membership, that
> savageness materialized in them and could be practised against those
> who did not share such membership. Had they abandoned it because
> it was 'abstract' to the point of lacking meaning or, on the contrary,
> because in that so-called 'abstraction' there was a symbolic value that
> went against the desire to dominate and possess others under the aegis
> of a national, racial, or ideological membership that was considered
> superior?[217]

It can hardly pass unnoticed that her argument goes clean against the
thesis, propounded by Lyotard and others, that there exists a direct
line of descent – or a 'genealogical' connection – between the tenets
and values of Enlightenment thought and the worst atrocities of
modern history, from Auschwitz to Hiroshima and the Gulag Archi-
pelago.[218] This case is most often made out in terms of a repressive
(monological or instrumental) reason that subjugates humanity and
nature alike to its drive for mastery and power. Of Nietzschean
extraction, it unites a wide range of New Historicist, Foucauldian
and post-structuralist thinkers. It is also to be found – albeit in more
qualified and subtly nuanced form – as a leading theme of the

'negative dialectic' that Adorno deployed against the claims of Hegelian and other such totalizing systems of thought.[219] But the current high vogue for notions of 'difference' and 'alterity' has nothing of Adorno's scrupulous care to conserve the critical resources of enlightened reason even while denouncing its perversion into forms of inhuman (unreflective) means-end rationality.

A similar objection can be raised against those – including the 'early' Kristeva – who look to Bakhtin as a primary source for the idea of a wholesale overturning of values (chiefly the values of reason, logic, and purposive agency) brought about by modes of 'carnevalesque' or anarchic libidinal abandon.[220] For here also there is a manifest failure to conceive how this radical-sounding rhetoric of transgression – of 'heteroglossia', parodic inversion, open-ended textual polyphony, and so forth – might actually connect with any substantive ethics or politics. Hence, as I have argued, the curious fact that Kristeva's chief nominees for the honour of having launched the revolution in poetic language make up such a motley (in some cases proto-fascist) company of thinkers and writers. After all, one has to ask whether the business of subverting established (constitutional) value-systems is *always and necessarily* a progressive act, or whether on some occasions – as for instance in Germany or Spain during the early 1930s, or again (more recently) in Chile, Nicaragua, and other beneficiaries of US-style 'freedom' and 'democracy' – it might not be aligned with the forces of reaction. Again, as with Foucault, it is the absence of an adequate normative dimension that renders such thinking prone to all the vagaries of a self-styled 'radicalism' devoid of any genuine ethical or political content. It is therefore understandable – though also, understandably, a cause of disarray among her erstwhile followers – that Kristeva should now see fit to invoke a whole series of classic liberal pronouncements on human rights, on the relationship between truth, reason, and justice, on the need for enlightened critique of existing social institutions, and on the universality of these values above and beyond the claims of localized cultural or ethnic difference. For post-structuralism and its offshoots had nothing to say – or nothing of ethical substance – that could offer some means of reflecting critically on the current resurgence of nationalist myths and regressive fundamentalist creeds. On the one hand it lacked any notion of the subject capable of bearing such a role. On the other it raised the rhetoric of 'difference' into a slogan whose political implications were at best obscure, and at worst a grim prognostic of recent events in ex-Yugoslavia and elsewhere.

Of course one may argue, like Stanley Fish, that 'theory' is an inconsequential activity; that it cannot do other than rhetorically endorse the views of some more-or-less widespread 'interpretive community'; and therefore that one might as well relinquish talk of reasons, principles, validating grounds etc. and settle for a straight-forward pragmatist appeal to what's good in the way of belief.[221] But this position looks plausible only if one starts out from some-thing like the post-structuralist premise that discourse (or rhetoric) goes 'all the way down', with the *consequence* – seemingly invisible to Fish – that henceforth all truth-claims and subject-positions must be viewed as relative to the language-game in question, and thus as mere products of suasive contrivance or localized cultural consensus. Once abandon this premise and the whole line of argument shows up as radically flawed. That is to say, there is no reason – aside from the 'linguistic turn' and its resultant forms of modish epistemological scepticism – to reject the much-derided commonsense view that language does very often refer to real-world states of affairs, and furthermore that truth-claims (including theoretical truth-claims) may indeed have real and decisive consequences for our conduct as reflective moral agents.

This was Aristotle's point when he argued that certain kinds of practical syllogism could issue not only in a further proposition but also in some appropriate action or mode of conduct equally con-sistent with the given premises.[222] Other philosophers – Stuart Hampshire among them – have likewise insisted on the close relation between ethical theory and practice, and on the fallacy involved in any thinking (like Hume's) that treats them as separate realms.[223] For such thinking itself has consequences, albeit of a negative and disabling kind. On the one hand it can lead to the notion of ethics as a higher-order (meta-linguistic) discipline whose business is to clarify the status or 'logical grammar' of our various moral conceptions, but not to address more substantive issues of justice, freedom, or rights. On the other – as in Hume and some latterday varieties of emotivist doctrine – it produces a generalized scepticism with regard to theory in whatever form, so that reason is regarded as a 'slave of the passions', and ethics reduces to a matter of moral sentiment without need for any further (reasoned or principled) justification.[224] One arrives at much the same position – *vide* Rorty – by pushing the linguistic turn to a point where high-toned talk about truth, justice, the 'political responsibility of the intellectuals', and so forth shows up as just another transient contender for the role of 'final vocabulary'. Nor has post-structuralism anything better to offer, having set its sights on the ultimate demise of all such delusive ('liberal-humanist') values. At least Fish's arguments have the propaedeutic merit of stating this outcome with firm (if cynical) conviction, and thus underlining the moral as well as the political bankruptcy of much that currently passes for advanced theoretical wisdom.

It is in this context that we need to evaluate Kristeva's very marked change of mind *vis-à-vis* the tradition of enlightened, 'cosmopolitan', or left-liberal thought. The following (on Kant) is a fair enough sample of the way that her writing typically passes over from what might appear non-committal paraphrase to a style that carries some considerable weight of implied or explicit endorsement.

> This is where the acknowledgment of *difference* is inscribed at the very heart of the universal republic. First, the *coexistence* of states will guarantee their vitality and their democracy better than 'amalgamation of states under one superior power', which might degenerate into one universal monarchy – a potential source of anarchy. Second, Nature, whom free practical reason respects and fulfils, 'employs two means to separate peoples and to prevent them from mixing: differences of language and of religion'. Thus *separation* and *union* would guarantee universal peace at the core of this cosmopolitanism, understood as coexistence of the differences that are imposed by the techniques of international relations on the one hand and political morality on the other. In short, since politics can only be moral, the fulfilment of man and of the designs of Providence demand that it be 'cosmopolitical'.[225]

One response to this passage – perhaps the likeliest response among those trained up on her earlier work – is that Kristeva must here be offering either a neutral summary of Kant's argument or a somewhat heavy-handed ironic rendition. What remains of 'difference', these readers might ask, if it is finally to be brought under the aegis of a 'universal republic' whose dictates are those of 'free practical reason' conceived in such overtly Enlightenment terms? How can this appeal to 'political morality' – to human rights and obligations, procedural justice, international law, indeed the whole panoply of liberal values – be squared with Kristeva's more 'radical' ideas as set out in her writings on language, desire, and difference? In short: shouldn't we take a lesson from Rorty and read this passage as a po-faced satire on 'honest old uncle Kant'?

Kristeva's next sentence should be enough to dispel such lingering suspicions. 'This reasoned hymn to cosmopolitanism', she writes,

> which runs through Kant's thought as a debt to Enlightenment and the French Revolution, appears indeed, today still, like an idealistic utopia, but also as an inescapable necessity in our contemporary universe, which unifies production and trade among nations at the same time as it perpetuates among them a state of war both natural and spiritual.[226]

And should any doubts remain then one need refer only to her admiring discussion of Montesquieu's *Spirit of the Laws* and the celebrated passage in which he reflects on justice in its private, its social or communal, and its wider (ethico-political) aspect.

> If I knew anything useful to myself and detrimental to my family, I would reject it from my mind. If I knew something useful to my family but not to my homeland, I would try to forget it. If I knew something useful to my homeland and detrimental to Europe, or else useful to Europe and detrimental to Mankind, I would consider it a crime.[227]

That she cites this passage twice over – on both occasions without the least hint of parodic or negative intent – is sufficient indication of the distance that Kristeva has travelled since a work like *The Revolution in Poetic Language*. In part this has to do with her vivid perception of the harms brought about by a rhetoric of cultural otherness, difference, or alterity that so easily translates into forms of ethnic hatred and racist paranoia. But it also goes along with a profound revaluation of the ethical resources – the potential for reflecting on our current sorry state of world-political affairs – held out by that tradition of liberal–enlightenment thought whose representative voices she assembles in *Strangers to Ourselves*. And if this means abandoning some of the main tenets of post-structuralist belief – the demise of truth, the dissolution of the subject, the raising of difference (or heterogeneity) to a high point of radical doctrine – then clearly it is a price that Kristeva is willing to pay.

Since her book first appeared (in 1988) its arguments have received the most appalling kind of negative confirmation. What occurred in many regions of ex-Yugoslavia is something like a retrograde version – a speeded-up sequence in reverse – of the speculative 'cosmopolitical' history envisaged by Kant and prefigured in the passage from Montesquieu cited above. From the break-up of the federal union it took just this short period of time for a handful of demagogues – Milosevic, Karadzic, and their like – to bring about a Hobbesian 'state of nature', a war of all against all in which erstwhile neighbours of notionally 'different' race, people who had long since forgotten those differences through community of custom and interest, were now reduced village by village to a state of suspicion, nascent paranoia, 'ethnic cleansing', mass-murder, and systematic rape. Nothing could more clearly illustrate Kristeva's point: that in the face of such continuing prospects of large-scale catastrophic regression Kant's thought represents not only an 'idealistic utopia' (that is to say, an idea of 'pure practical reason') but also an 'inescapable necessity' in our contemporary world. The great strength of her book is that it manages to sustain this alternative vision whilst giving full weight to those reactive forces – those mechanisms of paranoid projection – which blind us to the element of strangeness in ourselves and locate such strangeness only in the feared and hated other. From the Greek and Roman Stoics to the late ('meta-psychological') Freud there has existed a tradition of thought which has striven to reconcile this harsh knowledge with a sense of how it might yet be transformed into a source of renewed self-knowledge and tolerant regard for the variety of human values, beliefs, and social institutions. 'What might be involved, in the last analysis, is extending to the notion of *foreigner* the right of respecting our own foreignness and, in short, of the "privacy" that ensures freedom in democracies.'[228] But we shall not achieve this wished-for condition by fetishizing 'difference' to the point where it becomes a *ne plus ultra* of radical theory, a term whose indiscriminate usage very often brings it close to the active false logic of persecution-mania and a rhetoric of cultural *Apartheid*.

X

Of truth and falsehood in an extra-textual sense

One might recall, in this connection, Derrida's essay in tribute to Nelson Mandela.[229] His argument concerns Mandela's profession (or his ethical vocation) as a lawyer, one who moreover – before and during his imprisonment – exemplified the claims of a moral law transcending the perversions of legality and justice that characterized the South African state. Elsewhere, in a piece entitled 'Apartheid's Last Word', Derrida drew some strong criticism by appearing to treat that term as yet another item for rhetorical deconstruction, for ingenious dismantling in order to display its inbuilt 'aporias' or lack of determinate sense.[230] But if one reads these essays together – as I think they ought to be read – then it quickly becomes clear how wide of the mark is any critique of deconstruction that views it as merely a 'textualist' gambit for avoiding issues of real-world moral and political responsibility. What Derrida most admires (in 'Admiration: pour Nelson Mandela') is precisely the courage and intelligence displayed by one whose subjection to the rigours of an unjust and brutal state system prevented him neither from exerting his claims as an autonomous moral agent nor from condemning that system in the name of a higher, more enlightened tribunal.[231] It is the same essential point that Kristeva makes when she reminds us – *contra* the prevailing postmodernist wisdom – that the Nazis 'did not lose their humanity because of the "abstraction" that may have existed in the notion of "man" '. On the contrary (and her words might just as well apply to the South African instance) 'it is because they had lost the lofty, abstract, fully symbolic notion of humanity and replaced it with a local, national, or ideological membership that savageness materialized within them and could be practised against those who did not share such membership'.[232]

I have cited this passage once again for the light it sheds on Derrida's understanding of Mandela as a truly exemplary figure, an embodiment of 'free practical reason' in its role of resisting the false legality of a corrupt and oppressive socio-political order. For in his case also – as with those who stood out against the Nazi perversion of justice and morality – there was (in Kristeva's words) 'a symbolic value that went against the desire to dominate and possess others under the aegis of a national, racial, or ideological membership that was considered superior'.[233] The most crucial point here is that there is no contradiction between, on the one hand, acknowledging the fact of historical contingency – that we are born into situations not of our choosing – and on the other the principle that we should seek so far as possible to criticize and transform those conditions where they fall manifestly short of what is required of a just and equitable society. Again it finds expression in the few, densely summarized yet passionately argued pages that Kristeva devotes to Montesquieu's *Spirit of the Laws*. For here, as she writes,

> an *ideality* has been posited (the 'general spirit'), of which the stoic and Christian, natural and 'liberal' genealogy has been pointed out, and which is a fundamental prospect of Montesquieu's political thought. It at once endows it with its moral essence (as Kant clarified this notion in his conception of what he saw as the indissoluble pair constituted by the 'political' and the 'ethical') in that, beyond climatic determinations, for instance, it emphasizes a *contingency* in which both the course and the fatality of history are carried out, and in which the exercise of political freedom is precisely located.[234]

I have perhaps said enough to indicate how closely this corresponds to the values and principles invoked by Derrida in his essay on Mandela. In each case there is a twofold ground of appeal: to the individual conscience as arbiter of right and wrong, and, beyond that, to the wider community of judgment – the Kantian *sensus communis* – wherein such questions can intelligibly be raised *despite and against* the localized pressures of conformist (state-sponsored or naturalized) belief.

Such ideas may indeed be called 'utopian' in the sense that they find no actual location, no present or hitherto-existing example in the history of achieved social orders. Moreover, as postmodern cynics like Lyotard are fond of pointing out, there is a great deal of evidence – i.e., the whole catalogue of failed revolutions, post-

revolutionary terrors, pogroms, nationalist revivals, outbreaks of
renewed ethnic hatred, and so forth – to suggest that any 'cosmopolitical' hopes for a better future must indeed be confined to the
Kantian province of pure practical reason. And the record has hardly
improved since Lyotard composed his gloomy recitation.[235] If one
adds Yugoslavia to the list (along with Somalia, Iran and Iraq,
Nicaragua, El Salvador, Paraguay, Panama and other such
beneficiaries of a US-sponsored 'New World Order', Cuba looking
set to be the latest among them, as well as Northern Ireland, South
Africa, and East Timor *inter alia*) then it might seem that the balance-
sheet is beyond all hope of eventual redress. But Kristeva's argument
still holds, for reasons that Lyotard ought to have recognized, given
his constant (albeit highly slanted and heterodox) invocations of
Kant. For what is it if not the more enlightened alternative – Montesquieu's 'spirit of the laws' or the Kantian *sensus communis* – that
enables us to register these melancholy events as precisely an affront
to human hopes and aspirations, as instances of massive social and
political injustice, or as evidence that the progress toward a higher
('cosmopolitical') ideal may always be pushed into reverse by the
supervention of *Realpolitik* in some nationalist or geo-strategic
guise? And this applies just as much at the level of straightforward
personal and cultural attachment. 'To be sure', Montesquieu concedes, 'I love only my homeland.' Nevertheless, '[w]hen I travelled in
foreign countries, I became attached to them as to my own; I shared
in their lot, and I should have liked them to be in a flourishing
state'.[236] It is no great distance from this homely (yet not too homely)
reflection to Kristeva's more generalized commentary on it. 'The
nation's burden, so often acknowledged, is [thus] transposed in
order to be absorbed at the heart of a *borderless* political philosophy
dominated by the concern for politics understood as the maximal
integration of mankind in a moderate, attainable ideality.'[237] For it
is only in so far as thinking maintains this critical relation to existing
realities – 'utopian' in the positive (and philosophically acountable)
sense of that term – that ethics and politics resist the slide into forms
of acquiescent cynical wisdom.

     We are now better placed to understand why 'theory' (or the
version of it promoted by post-structuralists, Foucauldians, New
Historicists and others) has fallen in so readily with this current
counter-enlightenment trend. By 'decentring' the subject to the point
of non-existence – reducing it to a mere position within discourse or

a figment of the humanist Imaginary – post-structuralism has removed the very possibility of reasoned, reflective, and principled ethical choice. From Foucault comes the Nietzsche-inspired (but ultimately Hobbesian) notion that 'subjectivity' and 'subjection' are synonymous terms; that all truth-claims – including ethico-political ideas of reason – are reducible to effects of power/knowledge; and hence that we might as well abandon any hope of achieving progress through the exercise of reason in its enlightened (critical–emancipatory) role. New Historicism ends up by advocating much the same attitude, despite its methodological verve and its resourcefulness in conjuring novel relations between literary texts (canonical or otherwise) and all manner of so-called 'extraneous' source material. Where it joins the current litany of wanhope is in pushing this 'strong' intertextualist argument to the point of collapsing all generic distinctions between literary and other types of discourse, whether historical, philosophical, anthropological, or whatever. This way cultural solipsism lies. For it then fails to see – as I argued in comparing the typical New Historicist scene of colonial encounter with Kristeva's remarks about Montaigne – how scepticism (whether in regard to other minds, other cultures, or other sorts of text) produces just the kind of inherent circularity that locks understanding in a prison-house of its own contrivance. Indeed there is a sense in which the colonization of historiography by literary theory – or by 'radical' ideas imported from that field – can serve to obscure both the historical realities of colonial oppression and the experience of those who either suffered its effects or (like Montaigne) protested its injustice. Such is the upshot of a pan-textualist paradigm that leaves no room for the crucial difference between fact and fiction, truth-seeking narrative and the various modes of literary representation.

Elizabeth Fox-Genovese has noted this tendency in an essay that re-states certain simple truths against the high sophistication – not to say the sophistry – of New Historicism and sceptical historiographers like Hayden White. 'Contemporary critics', she writes,

> tend to insist disproportionately on history as the ways in which authors have written about the past at the expense of what might actually have happened, insist that history consists primarily of a body of texts and a strategy of reading and interpreting them. Yet history also consists, in a very old-fashioned sense, in a body of knowledge – in the sum of reliable information about the past that historians have

discovered and assembled. And beyond that knowledge, history must also be recognised as what did happen in the past – the social relations and, yes, 'events', of which our records offer only imperfect clues.[238]

Edward Said argues to similar effect when he remarks, in *Culture and Imperialism*, that it is difficult nowadays for clued-up Western intellectuals to offer any statement about history without first acknowledging Hayden White's thesis 'that all historical writing *is* writing and delivers figural language and representational tropes, be they in the modes of metonymy, metaphor, allegory, or irony'.[239] Meanwhile, altogether elsewhere, historians and scholars in the ex-colonial nations have a rather more urgent task to perform, one that leaves them no room for such luxuries of hyperinduced sceptical doubt. 'In the main', as Said concludes, 'the breach between these consequential metropolitan theorists and either the ongoing or the historical imperial experience is truly vast.'[240] Nor is this very remarkable if one considers the interests and priorities that such theorizing typically involves. For it is a capital irony, one not lost upon Said, that at a time when Western avant-garde theorists are busily rubbishing the Enlightenment and all its works, those same values should assume such importance for 'third-world' thinkers and activists striving to reclaim a history occluded by the hegemonic discourses of Western power.

I am aware that my using the term 'discourse' here might be seen as yet another symptom of the reflex habit – the textualist retreat into postures of high theoretical abstraction – which Said justifiably calls to account. In fact his own example is enough to make the point that it can be deployed to good, critically incisive effect on condition that its usage goes along with a sturdy sense of historical realities, an ethical commitment to truth, and a rejection of the facile (quasi-Derridean) idea that everything – history, philosophy, politics – comes down to just another 'kind of writing'. For one effect of this idea, most evident in New Historicism, is to level the distinction between factual and fictive (or assertoric and other, e.g. literary) modes of 'discourse', and hence to revoke that entire critical enterprise – from Spinoza on down – whose object has been to prevent such generic confusions.[241] In so doing, these current 'strong textualists' have reverted to a stage of pre-enlightenment belief when truth was equated with the meaning of scripture as vouchsafed to some authorized exegetes, fit though few, quite aside from all questions of historical veracity or standards of intelligible sense. And this despite the obvious objection that their readings espouse an attitude of thoroughgoing scepticism with regard to any 'transcendental signified', any appeal to theological or other such forms of overt doctrinal adherence. For it is among the more striking ironies of our 'postmodern' age that the widespread rejection of Enlightenment values like truth, reason, and critique has gone along with – and arguably contributed to – the resurgence of nationalist and religious fundamentalist creeds.

Some commentators (like Akbar Ahmed in his book *Postmodernism and Islam*) manifest a certain ambivalence toward this phenomenon, noting its dangers but refusing to judge them from a Western – i.e. enlightened, hence 'ethnocentric' – standpoint.[242] For Said, on the contrary, it is a melancholy fact that this retreat from the emancipatory values of modernity should be occurring both among Western intellectuals (or 'consequential metropolitan theorists') and those elsewhere who have everything to gain by conserving what is best in that tradition. 'We can and indeed must speculate', he writes,

as to why there has been a practice of self-confinement of the libertarian theoretical capital produced in the West, and why at the same time, in the formerly colonial world, the prospect for a culture with strongly liberationist components has rarely seemed dimmer.[243]

My point about New Historicism is that it mirrors this bilateral movement of retreat by reducing history to a textual construct – a projection of its own rhetorical and methodological concerns – and by thus treating the record of colonial encounters as a purely intra-discursive field of power/knowledge effects, quite aside from all issues of morality, conscience, or political justice. Hence, as I have argued, the very marked shift of emphasis in Said's work from *Orientalism* to *Culture and Imperialism*. For he is now clear that it is simply not enough to promote some alternative 'discourse' – some preferred rhetoric or different narrative version of events – by way of contesting the received colonialist wisdom. Rather, one has to point out how that received history has *falsified* the record, *suppressed* or *distorted* the relevant facts, and done so – moreover – *in bad faith* as an adjunct to the process of imperial subjection.

There are two aspects to this present-day *trahison des clercs*, the one having to do with its covert genealogy in the ruses and techniques of empire, the other with its failure to turn those lessons to a different, more positive or emancipatory account. Thus:

> [t]he contributions of empire to the arts of observation, description, disciplinary formation, and theoretical discourse have been ignored; and with fastidious discretion, perhaps squeamishness, these new theoretical discoveries have routinely bypassed the confluence between their findings and the liberationist energies released by resistance cultures in the Third World.[244]

Foucault and the New Historicists have had much to say – in negative-diagnostic mode – about those various techniques of surveillance, control, and 'disciplinary formation' that often (as in Orientalist discourse) claimed the title of 'enlightened' thought. But by adopting so bleak and sceptical a view they have failed to take stock of those genuine 'liberationist energies' that Said finds active in 'resistance cultures', and which are still conserved within the Enlightenment project as a standing tension between its critical impulse and its always implicit *promesse de bonheur*. If such ideas and values find no place in New Historicist writing then the reason is not far to seek. For on this account we must be utterly deluded – dupes of that outworn Enlightenment creed – if we look to the textual or documentary record in hope of discovering certain truths of human experience, whether with regard to the suffering inflicted by colonial oppression or the response of those, like Montaigne, who protested such injustice in the name of a higher (humanitarian or 'cosmopolitical') morality. Nothing could more clearly bring out the difference between a *scepticism* that questions religious and other forms of dogmatic or coercive truth-claim and a *cynicism* that treats all claims to truth – including those involved in the critique of revelation and the secularizing impulse of modernity – as equally unwarranted and pernicious in their effects.

New Historicism has boxed itself into this corner, following Foucault, through its extreme reaction against 'subject-centred' epistemologies and ethical values, and its consequent lack of any adequate normative dimension. But equally damaging is the textualist refusal – as remarked by Fox-Genovese in the passage I quoted above – to acknowledge any difference (or, as the pragmatists would have it, any 'difference that makes a difference') between historical fact and literary or fictive representation. For this distinction has been vital to the entire post-Renaissance enterprise of enlightened secular critique. I have written elsewhere about Spinoza's inaugural role in separating out the 'poetic' elements in scripture – those that responded to a reading in the metaphorical, allegorical, or figurative mode – from the various putative truth-claims whose mythic character was best revealed by the methods of comparative source-text analysis and reasoned historico-philological enquiry.[245] So it was, in William Empson's aptly irreverent phrase, that Christianity was 'knocked into civilized shape' through being brought to relinquish some of its more coercive methods for maintaining a monopoly on the discourse of revealed, self-validating truth.[246] But this hard-won progress was always liable to encounter setbacks, as when schools of neo-orthodox literary doctrine – like the American New Criticism – erected various quasi-theological sanctions around favoured tropes such as 'paradox', figures that were taken to rebuke the pretensions of mere human intellect or unaided secular reason.

There might seem little in common between that earlier movement and the latest (post-structuralist or New Historicist) vogues. After all, it was a leading tenet of the 'old' New Criticism – enounced most emphatically by its chief theoretician, W. K. Wimsatt – that poems should be treated as 'verbal icons', autonomous structures of inwrought verbal figuration foreclosing any appeal to history, biography, cultural context, or other such extraneous factors.[247] Hence those much-reviled 'heresies' (of paraphrase, intentionalism, scholarly source-hunting etc.) which were seen not only as a needless distraction from the sacrosanct 'words on the page' but also as a perilous confusion of realms, an opening of the text to all manner of reductive – e.g. secular or plain-prose rational – ideas. On the face of it no two positions could be more unlike than this stance of ontologically grounded aesthetic isolationism and the New Historicist will to subvert all those values invested in the literary text, along with the distinction between 'literature' itself and other (hitherto marginalized) forms of discourse. But on one point at least they converge: the belief that we can only be deluded – or in the grip of some naive misconception – if we think to gain access to truths of knowledge or experience beyond what is offered by their own techniques of high-powered textual exegesis. In this regard there is curiously little to choose between New Criticism's dogged insistence on respecting the autonomy of poetic form and New Historicism's gestures toward an open-ended intertextuality that would treat all writings as ontologically on a par and thus sweep away such value-laden categories as fact/fiction, history/literature, reality/ representation etc. What they both have in view – if for very different reasons – is a means to insulate the reading of texts from any 'outside' appeal to evidence or truth-claims that cannot be brought under the governing rubric of a generalized rhetoric or tropology.

For a critic like Wimsatt this meant drawing a *cordon sanitaire* around the literary text, such that poetry would not be subject to the kinds of intrusive rationalizing interest that others (Empson among them) displayed when they paraphrased poems or sought to analyse their structures of logico-semantic implication. In a late volume of essays – pointedly entitled *The Day of the Leopards* – Wimsatt mounted a rearguard defence of New Critical doctrine against these and other threats to the sovereign autonomy of poetic form.[248] Even so he can scarcely have envisaged that wholesale dissolution of generic boundaries that has become an article of faith for the current strong textualists. For it is now not poetry alone but *every* kind of 'discourse' – criticism, history, and philosophy included – which must be treated as rhetorical through and through, and hence as strictly off-limits for the purpose of reasoned or truth-seeking enquiry. Thus literary theory, through its colonizing drive into other disciplines, bids fair to reverse that entire movement of progressive or enlightened critique which has sought to establish adequate protocols for the discrimination of truth from falsehood, of factual from fictive or historical from mythic modes of utterance. If they are all just so many 'kinds of writing' (as Rorty says of philosophy) or optional modes of narrative emplotment (as in Hayden White's historiography) then clearly these distinctions must be given up, along with any ethical commitment to the values of truth and historical justice.

Perry Anderson has posed this question most forcefully with regard to recent 'revisionist' trends in writing about the Holocaust and subsequent events in German history.[249] He is concerned not only with the more egregious instances – outright denials that the Holocaust occurred or attempts to minimize the scale of atrocity – but also with arguments, like that of Andreas Hillgruber, which seek to 'recontextualize' the Holocaust by presenting it as one among several episodes of a comparably barbarous nature.[250] Thus for Hillgruber there is nothing either historically or ethically wrong about offering, as one such comparison, the post-war division of Germany and the Allies' 'betrayal' of the Eastern-bloc countries to the Soviet sphere of influence, resulting as it did in great human misery and the large-scale displacement of civilian populations. What are we to say when confronted with such arguments? Can it really be a matter (as Anderson asks, with a sidelong glance toward White and other sceptical historiographers) of suspending judgment, acknowledging the variety of possible narrative modes, and thus doing nothing to prejudice the issue between Hillgruber and his 'orthodox' opponents?

Such is the conclusion drawn by Lyotard when he discusses Robert Faurisson's outrageous thesis that for all we can know the gas-ovens at Auschwitz were never used for the mass extermination of Jewish and other victims since none of those victims has survived to verify the claim.[251] To which, one might think, there is a simple (but by no means simple-minded) line of response – that this is just a piece of sophistical chicanery, and that there exist many kinds of evidence besides that of first-hand documentary or ocular witness. But Lyotard replies – true to postmodernist form – by invoking his notion of the 'differend' as that which enjoins us to respect the heterogeneity of language-games, each disposing of its own *sui generis* criteria. In which case we have no right to criticize Faurisson on terms laid down by traditional modes of scholarly enquiry or good-faith historical research. For it is evident enough – on Lyotard's submission – that Faurisson simply doesn't accept those standards, and therefore that we do him a signal injustice by applying them to his statements about the Holocaust. More than that: we fall straight into Faurisson's trap by adopting a 'totalitarian' approach that takes for granted its own privileged status with regard to issues of truth, justice, and ethical accountability. For he can then justifiably retort that his opponents have made him the victim of a discourse that suppresses the narrative or speech-act differend, and which thus peremptorily denies his right to a free and fair hearing.

I have written elsewhere – and at greater length – about the confusions linguistic, philosophical, and moral that induce Lyotard to equate 'justice' with the suspension of reasoned or principled argument in matters of historical truth.[252] Nothing is more clearly indicative of the deep-laid cultural malaise that has taken hold with the turn against Enlightenment values and the consequent retreat into a postmodern rhetoric of difference, textuality, subject-positions, incommensurable phrase-regimes, and so forth. But the point is best made in a passage from Perry Anderson's essay on

Hillgruber which states these issues with much-needed clarity and force. 'What are the limits of a historical representation of Nazism and the Final Solution, through the prism of Hillgruber's work?' Anderson's answer gathers up many of the themes I have addressed in this essay so I make no apology for quoting the paragraph *in extenso*.

> Firstly, certain absolute limits are set by the evidence. Denial of the existence of either – of the regime, or its crimes – is plainly ruled out. No such issue arises in this case. Counter-factuals are also subject to control by the rules of evidence, which will eliminate some of them, as they do in this case. Narrative strategies, to be credible, always operate within *exterior* limits of this kind. Secondly, however, such narrative strategies are in turn subject to a double *interior* limitation. On the one hand, certain kinds of evidence preclude certain sorts of emplotment – the Final Solution cannot *historically* be written as romance, or comedy. On the other hand, any generic emplotment has only a weak determinative power over the selection of evidence. Hillgruber could legitimately depict the end of East Prussia as tragic; however, that choice, permitted by the evidence, did not in itself dictate the series of particular empirical judgements that make up his account of it. There is a large gap between genre and script. Other, divergent, tragic accounts could be written of the same events – and these would not be incommensurable forms, or so many fictions, but epistemologically discriminable attempts to reach the truth. The typical measure of such discrimination is not the presence of *suggestio falsi*, very rare in modern historiography, but the degree of *suppressio veri* – that is, representation omitted rather than misrepresentation committed. In history, as in the sciences, the depth of a truth is usually a function of its width – how much of the evidence it engages and explains.[253]

In a sense (as Anderson would surely concede) this passage does no more than render explicit the various working assumptions, implied axiomatics, interpretive protocols, and so forth that are taken for granted in the writing and reading of historical texts. That is, it simply states – in more 'technical' form – the preconditions for what should count as historical discourse and also (symmetrically) for what should count as a competent or good-faith reading thereof.

Needless to say, those assumptions have lately come under attack from various quarters. The challenge has been mounted on the one hand by theorists in the Nietzschean line of descent (post-structuralists, Foucauldians, sceptical tropologists like Hayden

White), and on the other by writers – novelists and historians – who create hybrid genres with the object of similarly blurring the line between historical and fictive modes of utterance. These latter are most usefuly surveyed by Linda Hutcheon under the capacious rubric of 'historiographic metafiction'.[254] On the fictional side – in so far as that term still applies – it would include the work of novelists like Kurt Vonnegut, D. M. Thomas, E. L. Doctorow, Thomas Pynchon, and Jeanette Winterson. Among historians one thinks of Simon Schama – especially his recent book *Dead Certainties* – and also of the turn towards anecdotal narrative (combined with techniques of ethnographic 'thick description') in writers like Robert Darnton and Jonathan Spence.[255]

All of this might seem to pose a huge problem for any attempt – like Anderson's – to reassert the difference between truth and falsehood, history and fiction, or factual and counterfactual (speculative) modes of historically oriented enquiry. But it will so appear, I would venture to suggest, only from the standpoint of theorists more acquainted with high postmodernist lore than with the reading of texts (like those I have mentioned above) that contrive to inhabit this complex generic domain. For what such reading involves is a constant process of adjustment, a passage back and forth – sometimes from sentence to sentence – across and between the various modalities of historical and fictive discourse. And this applies whether the text in question is a novel that incorporates elements of history (like Doctorow's *Ragtime* or Vonnegut's *Slaughterhouse Five*) or a work of historical narration (such as Schama's) which self-consciously aims to subvert or 'deconstruct' the more orthodox conventions of the genre. In neither case are we simply at a loss to tell the difference, unless (of course) we lack all knowledge of the relevant history, or deliberately set such knowledge aside in pursuit of some wholesale sceptical doctrine.

No doubt there are numerous problematic cases – sometimes turning up in pairs, like Orwell's *Homage to Catalonia* and Hemingway's *For Whom the Bell Tolls* – where the fact/fiction boundary is especially fuzzy, so that commentators (historians and literary critics) continue to engage in borderline disputes. But these are exceptions that prove the rule, the rule being that we can and do manage to find our way around these complex ontological issues, often (be it said) with greater success than those theorists – whether postmodern sceptics or proponents of a more-or-less qualified realist approach – who address such questions in the abstract. Not that theory is itself without resources in this matter. One line of thought, among philosophers and literary critics alike, has involved the application of modal logic and the idea of a plurality of 'possible worlds' wherein certain features of past or present (this-worldly) reality are either conserved with respect to their truth-values, taken as holding across the ontological divide, or subjected to various kinds and degrees of precisely specified alteration.[256] This approach has the merit of helping to explain, in Perry Anderson's words, how 'divergent accounts could be written of the same events', even though 'these would not be aesthetically incommensurable forms, or so many fictions, but epistemologically discriminable attempts to reach the truth'. At any rate it offers a more promising option than those other (post-structuralist or textualist) theories which count 'reality' a world well lost and 'truth' just a cover-term to mask the operations of an all-pervasive epistemic will-to-power. For the result of such thinking, if consistently pursued, is to undermine every last standard of scholarly, critical, and ethical accountability.

Terry Lovell makes a similar point – also with reference to revisionist treatments of the Holocaust – when remarking on the consequences of a thoroughgoing discourse-relativism as applied to questions of historical truth.

> A history of the Third Reich which made no mention of the murder of six million Jews would be felt by most people to be seriously inadequate. Is this only because we are erroneously comparing this discourse about the Third Reich with other discourses which happen to contain among their objects 'extermination camps', 'gas chambers', 'pogroms' etc.? Or is it because such discourses are quite properly referred to a world of real objects in which these things really existed, and not just internally to their own logic?[257]

Lovell is here alluding to the post-Marxist (more precisely: the post-Althusserian) version of discourse-relativism espoused by Barry Hindess and Paul Hirst.[258] But these remarks are just as relevant to that whole contemporary movement of thought – anti-realist, ultra-sceptical, counter-enlightenment, opposed to all normative values or truth-claims – for which 'postmodernism' serves as the most compendious descriptive term.

If one asks how this attitude has taken such a hold among large sections of the present-day 'radical' intelligentsia then the answer is evident enough. It has come about through the lack of any reasoned or principled resistance among thinkers convinced – on post-structuralist grounds – that the subject is nothing more than a side-effect of 'discourse', a nominal entity or mirage of the humanist imaginary. For what we are left with then is a range of multiple but always pre-constituted 'subject-positions', none of which affords the least prospect of exerting any independent effort of thought, any will to raise questions of truth or justice except in so far as those questions take rise from some in-place (purely strategic) conjunction of power/knowledge interests. Nor are the current alternatives very much better when, as often happens, they start out from this same *a priori* persuasion – that is to say, from some variant of the linguistic or textualist turn – and seek to pass 'beyond' it while leaving its major premises firmly in place. Such are those vacuous appeals to an ethics or a politics of radical 'difference' which – whether couched in Levinasian or in New Historicist terms – always end up by constructing the 'other' as an empty, unthinkably alien position within discourse whose lineaments can only be descried in the image of the theorist's own concerns.

Carolyn Porter argues to similar effect in a recent, combative but well-argued essay on the New Historicism. As she sees it this movement might better be called 'Colonialist Formalism' on account of its tendency first to appropriate some striking anecdote or scene of colonial encounter, then to textualize that scene through a rhetorical strategy of containment that allows no voice – no active or participant role – to the historical agents concerned. 'I am suggesting', she writes,

> that insofar as New Historicist work relies upon the anecdotalization of the discursive field now opened for interpretation, it can only expand the range of the very formalism which it so manifestly wants to challenge . . . [It] can treat the social text in much the same way it has been accustomed to treating the literary one, that is, as the scene of tension, paradox, and ambiguity. Further, it is not only marginal groups and subordinated cultures that can be occulted, whether by exclusion or incorporation, by effacement or appropriation, but the 'social' itself as well. Insofar as this happens, the 'social text' remains a text in the formalist sense, rather than the literary being historicized as itself a form of social discourse.[259]

If history can thus be transformed into yet more grist for the textualist mill then the same applies to those ethical modulations –

those appeals to absolute otherness, difference, heterogeneity, and so forth – which have lately been invoked as a high-toned alibi for theorists in quest of some opening beyond the post-structuralist prison-house of discourse. Such an opening is simply not available, I have argued, so long as they persist in the dogma that subjectivity, knowledge, and experience are relative to (or 'constructed in') language, and hence that genuine respect for the other must entail casting doubt upon everything that enables us to respond or communicate across and between cultures. Seldom in the history of thought – theology aside – can so much ingenious endeavour have yielded so little in the way of humane understanding or improved interpretative grasp. But there are heartening signs, in the recent work of thinkers like Kristeva and Said, that this orthodoxy is meeting a vigorous challenge from some of those once routinely enlisted in its name.

Postscript:
'The undefined work of freedom'
– Foucault and philosophy

Michel Foucault had no wish to be considered a 'philosopher' in any conventional (academically recognized) sense of that term. Much of his work was indeed devoted to a radical contestation of philosophy, or what Foucault saw as its complicitous role in upholding disciplinary regimes of instituted power/knowledge. In his early writings (notably *Les mots et les choses*, 1966) this resistance took the form of a critical 'archaeology', a questing-back for the various discourses, paradigms, or structures of representation that had constituted 'knowledge' and 'truth' down through the history of post-Renaissance thought.[260] His argument, briefly stated, was that the modern human sciences (philosophy among them) had emerged through a series of shifting configurations in the order of discourse, this passage being marked by successive ruptures – or 'epistemological breaks' – where one such regime gave way to another. Thus Renaissance thinking was founded on the notions of resemblance, analogy, or symbolic correspondence, its dominant metaphor that of the 'great book of nature' wherein God's signature was everywhere legible. The subsequent epoch (roughly speaking, from the mid sixteenth to the mid eighteenth century) saw the rise of a classical discourse whose governing metaphors were taxonomic or classificatory, and whose sciences – geology, botany, economics (or the 'analysis of wealth'), linguistics, anthropology etc. – all bore witness to this common concern with establishing a grid-like morphology of genus and species.

With the next major shift, so Foucault contends, a 'profound historicity entered the heart of things', displacing those synchronic categories and ushering in principles of change, evolution, dialectics, organic development, purposive historical agency, etc. Moreover this was an age that found its inaugural moment in the project of Kantian ('enlightened') critique, in that figment of the humanist imaginary – the knowing, willing, and judging subject – whose transcendental status Kant strove to demonstrate, and whose imminent demise Foucault famously evoked in his simile of man as a figure drawn in sand at the ocean's edge, soon to be erased by the incoming tide. For we were now living through the terminal phase of that same anthropocentric discourse, its dissolution signalled by the advent of *language* as the ultimate horizon – the limit-point or condition of possibility – for the so-called 'human sciences'. Among its portents, according to Foucault, were Symbolist poetry (Mallarmé's in particular), the effects of linguistic *mise-en-abîme* created by experimental writers like Raymond Roussel, and the structuralist turn across manifold disciplines – from anthropology to philosophy and literary criticism – that followed from the pioneering work of Saussure. These developments had all laid siege to man, that strange 'transcendental–empirical doublet' of Kant's delusory conception whose figure would now merge back into the fabric of a discourse that effaced his very memory. In short, Foucault rejected Kant's claim to have brought about a 'Copernican revolution' in philosophy, a critique of those anthropological residues that had characterized his own previos thinking. For the 'transcendental subject' was itself nothing more than a transient fold in the order of discourse, a space briefly filled – and soon to be vacated – by that self-same specular mirage.

One can find a further motive for Foucault's deep resistance to philosophy in books like *The Birth of the Clinic, Madness and Civilization*, and *Discipline and Punish*.[261] Here he argues that the truth-claims of philosophic reason – and especially those of the Cartesian *cogito* – have always gone along with an obsessive desire to police its own boundaries by excluding whatever is currently perceived as mad, abnormal, deviant, criminal, perverse, etc. At times this exclusion has assumed a highly visible and overtly repressive aspect, as in episodes like the 'Great Confinement' of the mid seventeenth century, or in penal practices – like torture, mutilation, or public execution – by which the dictates of judicial authority or sovereign power were very literally inscribed upon the body of the suffering miscreant. But we are wrong, Foucault argues, to count it a sign of our superior ('enlightened') dispensation that such practices are no longer tolerated, that psychiatric treatment has taken the place of other, more 'barbarous' disciplinary regimes, or that nowadays the social and welfare services have taken over much of the work once performed by corporal punishment or repressive state institutions. On the contrary: these new 'technologies of the self' have a power to reach into our most intimate 'private' thoughts and desires unmatched by their older and cruder counterparts. For at this point the operations of power/knowledge pass over from the realm of external discipline to the realm of inward (e.g. confessional, spiritual, or psychoanalytic) scrutiny where the subject willingly consents to such forms of self-imposed surveillance and control. It is a prospect that Foucault finds aptly figured in Bentham's now notorious 'Panopticon', his notion of an ideal prison so designed – on a circular pattern with the cells facing inward and open to view – that the convicts would feel themselves always subject to a omnipresent gaze which dispensed with the need for elaborate security measures. Such would be the ultimate 'carceral society', the outcome of a project (call it 'enlightenment' or the 'philosophic discourse of modernity') which Foucault equates with the drive towards ever more effective and subtilized forms of 'voluntary' self-discipline.

In his middle-period writings – roughly, from 1965 to 1975 – Foucault turned to Nietzsche as (alone among the philosophers) a kindred spirit, a 'genealogist' of power/knowledge who had likewise exposed the inveterate will-to-power that masked behind talk of 'reason' and 'truth'.[262] For him, as for Nietzsche, such effects could be resisted only by adopting a stance of out-and-out epistemological scepticism, coupled with an ultra-nominalist view of 'truth' as a purely rhetorical construct, and – following from this – an antinomian ethics aimed towards the ceaseless 'transvaluation' of established truth-claims and values. But in the decade or so before his early death Foucault showed signs of moving away from this resolutely Nietzschean position. The change appears to have occurred during the course of his work towards the four-volume *History of Sexuality*, and was clearly visible in the articles and interviews collected for posthumous publication. Volume One of the *History* is mainly concerned to discredit what he calls the 'repressive hypothesis', the idea that sexuality was once subject to all manner of (e.g.) 'Victorian' constraints and taboos, but that now, having become more enlightened in such matters, we can talk openly about sexual hang-ups – on the psychiatrist's couch or elsewhere – and thus win through to a freedom undreamt of by our less fortunate ancestors.[263]

What this ignores, on Foucault's account, is the aspect of *compulsion* that is always bound up with the need to confess, to articulate our every last thought, motive, and desire, and thus submit ourselves ('willingly' enough) to the imperious order of discourse. But in subsequent volumes – *The Use of Pleasure* and *The Care of the Self* – Foucault modifies this position at least to the extent of acknowledging that we need to reconstruct a more *truthful* genealogy of morals, of erotic and ethical conduct, which will trace the 'history of the present' from Greek and Roman antiquity, through the Christian confessional, to Freudian psychiatry and other such modes of sexual knowledge-production.[264] And this can be achieved only in so far as we recognize first the claims of accurate (truth-seeking) scholarship, and second our shared human interest in dispelling the sources of imaginary misrecognition and attaining a better, more informed or adequate sense of that formative pre-history. In these late writings, as Foucault says, 'a whole morality is at stake, a morality that concerns the search for the truth and the relation to the other'.[265]

Most striking in this regard is the essay 'What Is Enlightenment?', a text that not only borrows its title from Kant but finds Foucault adopting a very different attitude to the Kantian values of truth, autonomy, and enlightened self-knowledge.[266] It is still – I should add – a heterodox reading, one that sets out to shift argumentative terrain by pairing Kant (improbably enough) with a poet like Baudelaire, and thus re-defining 'modernity' in relation to the discourse of aesthetic self-fashioning, rather than that of philosophical critique. But taken together with his other late works it shows just how far Foucault had travelled from the idea of truth as nothing more than a ruse in the service of an epistemic will-to-power over minds and bodies alike. What he now discovers in the Kantian project is a moment whose uniqueness in the history of thought has to do with its opening a wholly new space for critical reflection on the scope and limits of our freedom. 'How are we constituted as subjects of our own knowledge? How are we constituted as subjects who exercise or submit to power relations? How are we constituted as moral subjects of our own actions?'[267] No longer can such issues be consigned, as in *Les mots et les choses*, to the status of pseudo-problems thrown up by a mere local perturbation in the sovereign order of discourse.

Of course there is a difference – a marked shift of emphasis – between Foucault's way of formulating these questions and Kant's brief statement of his own main concerns in the three *Critiques* ('What can I know? What ought I to do? What can I reasonably hope for?').

Thus Foucault still rejects – or at any rate resists – any form of the Kantian appeal to conditions of possibility (or transcendental grounds) for establishing the terms of enlightened, good-faith debate. And he still follows Nietzsche (up to a point) in asking not so much what is truly the case about ourselves as knowing, willing, and judging subjects, but rather what has brought it about – what formative events in our own 'enlightened' pre-history – that we should now see fit to pose such questions. But he also makes it clear, as against his earlier position, that without some regulative idea of truth (and also of *critique* as its enabling condition) there is no possibility of linking these issues to an ethics and a politics possessed of genuine emancipatory values. This critique, Foucault writes,

> will be genealogical in the sense that it will not deduce from the form of what we are what it is impossible for us to do and to know; but it will separate out, from the contingency that has made us what we are, the possibility of no longer being, doing, or thinking what we are, do, or think.[268]

As I have said, there remain some unresolved tensions in Foucault's late move toward a partial *rapprochement* with Kant. Chief among them is his desire – shared with postmodernists like Richard Rorty – to aestheticize ethics by construing 'autonomy' as a matter of private self-fashioning, a project carried on (or so it would seem) in virtual isolation from what Kant conceived as the public realm of collectively articulated reasons, motives, and interests.[269] All the same there are passages, like those cited above, where Foucault seems to qualify his earlier (Nietzschean) stance with regard to the ubiquity of power/knowledge, the obsolescence of Enlightenment reason, and the truth-claims of philosophy as merely a species of coercive disciplinary control. Thus:

> the thread that may connect us with the Enlightenment is not faithfulness to doctrinal elements, but rather the permanent reactivation of an attitude – that is, of a philosophical ethos that could be described as a permanent critique of our historical era.[270]

This passage is entirely in the spirit of Kant's original essay, not least as regards its commitment to 'permanent critique' and its rejection of mere doctrinal adherence as a measure of enlightened thought. (So Kant's great injunction *Sapere aude!* – 'Have the courage to know' – is not, as sceptics have sometimes argued, a directive that instructs us what to think and hence a kind of performative contradiction.)

I have assembled just a few of the many indications, in his last essays and interviews, that Foucault had come around to a changed estimate of philosophy's role *vis-à-vis* the interests of enlightened human understanding. It is only the bugbear notion of 'enlightenment' put about by postmodern commentators – the idea of a monolithic discourse bent upon suppressing all signs of cultural difference – that has led them to ignore this decisive shift of intellectual and ethical priorities. Certainly he had travelled a long way since those pages on Kant in *Les mots et les choses*, pages whose undoubted rhetorical brilliance went along with some distinctly wire-drawn argumentation. In his final interview with Paul Rabinow in May 1984 Foucault makes it clear just why he had abandoned the position taken up in both his early ('archaeological') and his middle-period ('genealogical') writings. 'Thought is not what inhabits a certain conduct and gives it meaning.' Rather, he suggests, it is 'what allows one to step back from this way of acting or reacting, to present it to oneself as an object of thought and question it as to its meaning, its conditions, and its goals'.[271] Such critical reflection would be strictly inconceivable – yet another figment of the obsolete humanist imaginary – on the set of assumptions that had characterized Foucault's previous work, that is to say, the post-structuralist view of language (or 'discourse') as the absolute horizon and condition of possibility for thought in general. If indeed it is the case that all truth-claims and subject-positions are inscribed within a pre-existent discourse, then clearly one cannot 'step back' from that discourse in order to criticize its 'meaning, its conditions, and its goals.'

So when Foucault returns to the reading of Kant in an essay like 'What Is Enlightenment?' it is with a view to reopening certain crucial issues – notably the relation between epistemology and ethics, or the Kantian modalities of knowing, willing, and judging – which up to then his work had scarcely entertained, or which he had treated as just one episode in the history of transient discourse-formations. Not that those issues had ever been entirely suppressed, even during his 'archaeological' phase when Foucault went about as far as possible in this direction. Indeed they were raised all the more sharply – though nowhere acknowledged as such – by the conflict between Foucault's express methodological commitments and his idea that resistance might somehow come about through the willed transgression of societal norms. Nor was this conflict in any way resolved by his switching to an overtly Nietzschean register, a rhetoric that situated meaning and truth within the force-field of contending power/knowledge interests. For this still left Foucault bereft of any adequate answer when it came to explaining on what possible grounds – factual, historical, ethical, or socio-political – one should wish to oppose some existing discourse in the name of some arguably better alternative. Another consequence, visible in much postmodern and post-structuralist theorizing, was the tendency to invest language itself with certain quasi-human or anthropomorphic attributes. Thus talk of the 'subject' – now regarded as the source of all transcendental illusions – was surreptitiously replaced with more up-to-date talk of discursive strategies, contests of meaning, resistant or multiple 'subject-positions', and so forth.

This throws (to say the least) an oddly revealing light on Foucault's claims in *Les mots et les choses* with regard to the anthropological residues in Kant's critical philosophy. The charge indeed comes back like a boomerange when Foucault treats questions of ethico-political agency on what amounts to a Hobbesian principle of the *bellum omnium contra omnes*, transposed (via Nietzsche) into a doctrine of language as the site of unending – if endlessly 'decentred' – struggles for power. Nothing could more clearly illustrate the ultimate dead-end to which theory is destined when it pushes the linguistic (or post-structuralist) turn to this point of terminal aporia. Hence Foucault's stress, in the interview with Rabinow, on the irreducibility of 'thought' to 'language', or the space that opens up for critical thinking *despite and against* the discurisve self-images of age. 'The work of philosophical and historical reflection is put back into the field of the work of thought only on condition that one clearly grasps problematization not as an arrangement of representations but as a work of thought.'[272] The very awkwardness of phrasing, in this and other passages, bears witness to the difficulty that Foucault experienced in his effort to wrest a domain of human agency, commitment, and choice from the prison-house logic of linguistic determinism. But of the need for such thinking he had no doubt, especially after the strenuous sequence of visions and revisions that had arisen out of his ten-year period of research towards the *History of Sexuality*. After all, as he pointedly remarked to Rabinow, 'by asking this sort of ethico-epistemologico-political question, one is not taking up a position on a chessboard'.[273] It is among the great losses of recent intellectual history that Foucault's work was cut short just as he embarked on this profound revaluation of his own project to date.

References

1 The literature is vast (and vastly uneven) but see for instance Thomas Docherty (ed.), *Postmodernism: a reader* (Hemel Hempstead: Harvester-Wheatsheaf, 1993); Ben Agger, *The Decline of Discourse: reading, writing and resistance in postmodern capitalism* (London: Falmer, 1990); Jonathan Arac (ed.), *Postmodernism and Politics* (Minneapolis: University of Minnesota Press, 1986); Alex Callinicos, *Against Postmodernism: a Marxist critique* (Cambridge: Polity Press, 1989); Steven Connor, *Postmodernist Culture: an introduction to theories of the contemporary* (Oxford: Basil Blackwell, 1989); David Harvey, *The Condition of Postmodernity: an enquiry into the origins of social change* (Oxford: Basil Blackwell, 1989); Linda Hutcheon, *The Politics of Postmodernism* (London: Routledge, 1989); Henry S. Kariel, *The Desperate Politics of Postmodernism* (Amherst, Mass.: University of Massachusetts Press, 1989); Hilary Lawson and Lisa Appignanesi (eds), *Dismantling Truth: reality in the postmodern world* (London: Weidenfeld & Nicolson, 1989); John McGowan, *Postmodernism and its Critics* (Ithaca, NY: Cornell University Press, 1991); Christopher Norris, *What's Wrong with Postmodernism: critical theory and the ends of philosophy* (Hemel Hempstead: Harvester-Wheatsheaf, 1989) and *The Truth about Postmodernism* (Oxford: Basil Blackwell, 1993); Andrew Ross (ed.), *Universal Abandon?: the politics of postmodernism* (Edinburgh: Edinburgh University Press, 1988); Michael J. Shapiro, *Reading the Postmodern Polity: political theory as textual practice* (Minneapolis: University of Minnesota Press, 1992); Mas'ud Zavarzadeh and Donald Morton (eds), *Theory, (Post) Modernity, Opposition* (Washington, DC: Maisonneuve Press, 1991); Stephen K. White, *Political Theory and Postmodernism* (Cambridge: Cambridge University Press, 1991).

2 See Ernesto Laclau and Chantal Mouffe, *Hegemony and Socialist Strategy: towards a radical democratic politics* (London: Verso, 1985); also Laclau, *New Reflections on the Revolution in Our Time* (London: Verso, 1990).

3 Jacques Derrida, 'The Principle of Reason: the university in the eyes of its pupils', trans. Catherine Porter and Edward P. Morris, *Diacritics*, Vol. XIII, No. 3 (1983), pp. 3–20; p. 20.

4 Perry Anderson, *Considerations on Western Marxism* (London: New Left Books, 1976).

5 For a fine synoptic survey, see Fredric Jameson, *Marxism and Form* (Princeton, NJ: Princeton University Press, 1971).

6 See Francis Barker *et al.* (eds), *Essex Conferences on the Sociology of Literature* (Colchester: University of Essex, 1976–81).

7 For the most influential statement of this case, see Jean-François Lyotard, *The Postmodern Condition: a report on knowledge*, trans. Geoff Bennington and Brian Massumi (Manchester: Manchester University Press, 1984); also Lyotard, *Political Writings*, ed. & trans. Bill Readings and Kevin Paul Geiman (London: UCL Press, 1993); *Peregrinations* (New York: Columbia University Press, 1988); and *The Lyotard Reader*, ed. Andrew Benjamin (Oxford: Basil Blackwell, 1989).

8 See Thomas Docherty, *After Theory: postmodernism/postmarxism* (London: Routledge, 1990).

9 See especially Louis Althusser, *For Marx*, trans. Ben Brewster (London: Allen Lane, 1969) and '*Philosophy and the Spontaneous Philosophy of the Scientists' and Other Essays*, ed. & trans. Gregory Elliott (London: Verso, 1990); also Elliott, *Althusser: the detour of theory* (London: Verso, 1987); Ted Benton, *The Rise and Fall of Structural Marxism* (London: Macmillan, 1984); and E. Ann Kaplan and Michael Sprinker (eds), *The Althusserian Legacy* (London: Verso, 1993).

10 For a survey and polemical critique, see my book *Uncritical Theory: postmodernism, intellectuals and the Gulf War* (London: Lawrence & Wishart and Amherst, Mass.: University of Massachusetts Press, 1992); also Stuart Sim, *Beyond Aesthetics: confrontations with postmodernism and post-structuralism* (Hemel Hempstead: Harvester-Wheatsheaf, 1992).

11 These developments receive a more favourable estimate in Docherty, *Beyond Theory* and Antony Easthope, *British Post-Structuralism Since 1968* (London: Routledge, 1988).

12 See Richard Rorty, *Contingency, Irony, and Solidarity* (Cambridge: Cambridge University Press, 1989) and *Objectivity. Relativism, and Truth* (Cambridge University Press, 1991). For some interesting discussion of this and related issues, see also Anindita Niyogi Balslev, *Cultural Otherness: correspondence with Richard Rorty* (Shimla, India: Indian Institute of Advanced Study, 1991). Roy Bhaskar, *Philosophy and the Idea of Freedom* (Oxford: Basil Blackwell, 1991) offers the most detailed critique of Rortian neo-pragmatism from an epistemological and ethico-political standpoint.

13 See for instance Clifford Geertz, *Local Knowledge: further essays on interpretive anthropology* (New York: Basic Books, 1983); Richard Rorty (ed.), *The Linguistic Turn: recent essays in philosophical method* (Chicago: University of Chicago Press, 1967); and Kenneth Baynes, James Bohman, and Thomas McCarthy (eds), *After Philosophy: end or transformation?* (Cambridge, Mass.: MIT Press, 1987).

14 Jürgen Habermas, *The Philosophical Discourse of Modernity: twelve lectures,* trans. Frederick W. Lawrence (Cambridge: Polity Press, 1987).

15 See W. V. O. Quine, *'Ontological Relativity' and Other Essays* (New York: Columbia University Press, 1969) and *Theories and Things* (Cambridge, Mass.: Harvard University Press, 1981).

16 Joseph Needham, *Science and Civilization in China* (nine vols to date, Cambridge: Cambridge University Press, 1954–88); see also Colin A. Ronan (ed.), *The Shorter 'Science and Civilization'* (Cambridge, 1978).

17 See Thomas S. Kuhn, *The Structure of Scientific Revolutions,* 2nd edn, and *The Essential Tension: selected studies in scientific tradition and change* (Chicago: University of Chicago Press, 1970 and 1977); Paul K. Feyerabend, *Against Method: outline of an anarchist theory of knowledge* (London: New Left Books, 1978) and *Farewell to Reason* (London: Verso, 1987).

18 Paisley Livingston, *Literary Knowledge: humanistic inquiry and the philosophy of science* (Ithaca, NY: Cornell University Press, 1988).

19 Lyotard, *The Postmodern Condition,* p. 60. See also Stuart Peterfreund (ed.), *Literature and Science: theory and practice* (Boston: Northeastern University Press, 1990) and James Gleick, *Chaos: making a new science* (New York: Viking Books, 1987).

20 See Feyerabend, *Farewell to Reason.*

21 I. A. Richards, *Principles of Literary Criticism* (London: Kegan Paul, Trench & Trubner, 1926).

22 See for instance the essays collected in Richards, *Speculative Instruments* (London: Routledge & Kegan Paul, 1955) and *Complementarities* (Cambridge, Mass.: Harvard University Press, 1976).

23 William Empson, *Seven Types of Ambiguity* (London: Chatto & Windus, 1930) and *Collected Poems* (London: Chatto & Windus, 1955).

24 Empson, *The Structure of Complex Words* (London: Chatto & Windus, 1951).

25 See Derrida, 'White Mythology: metaphor in the text of philosophy', in *Margins of Philosophy,* trans. Alan Bass (Chicago: University of Chicago Press, 1982), pp. 207–71 and 'The *Retrait* of Metaphor', *Enclitic,* Vol. II, No. 2 (1978), pp. 5–33. See also Christopher Norris, *Derrida* (London: Fontana, 1987).

26 Michel Foucault, *Folie et déraison: Histoire de la folie à l'age classique*

(Paris: Plon, 1961). An abridged English version appeared as *Madness and Civilization: a history of insanity in the age of reason*, trans. Richard Howard (New York: Pantheon, 1965). For Derrida's critique of Foucault, see 'Cogito and the History of Madness', in *Writing and Difference*, trans. Alan Bass (London: Routledge & Kegan Paul, 1978), pp. 31–63; also Roy Boyne, *Foucault and Derrida: the other side of reason* (London: Unwin Hyman, 1990).

27 See Habermas, *The Philosophical Discourse of Modernity*.

28 Jean-François Lyotard, *The Differend: phrases in dispute*, trans. Georges van den Abbeele (Manchester: Manchester University Press, 1988).

29 Habermas, *The Philosophical Discourse of Modernity*.

30 See Rorty, *Contingency, Irony, and Solidarity*.

31 I have attempted to provide such a range of counter-arguments in Norris, *Uncritical Theory* and *The Truth About Postmodernism*.

32 Rorty, *Consequences of Pragmatism* (Minneapolis: University of Minnesota Press, 1982), pp. 37–59.

33 Rorty, 'Overcoming the Tradition: Heidegger and Dewey', in *Consequences*, pp. 37–59.

34 Rorty, 'Moral Identity and Private Autonomy: the case of Foucault', in *Essays on Heidegger and Others* (Cambridge: Cambridge University Press, 1991), pp. 193–8.

35 See Rorty, *Philosophy and the Mirror of Nature* (Princeton, NJ: Princeton University Press, 1980).

36 Hilary Putnam, *Realism and Reason* (Cambridge: Cambridge University Press, 1983); also *Representation and Reality* and *Realism with a Human Face* (Cambridge, Mass.: Harvard University Press, 1988 and 1990).

37 Donald Davidson, 'On the Very Idea of a Conceptual Scheme', in *Inquiries into Truth and Interpretation* (Oxford: Clarendon Press, 1984), pp. 183–98.

38 *Ibid.*, p. 184.

39 *Ibid.*, p. 195.

40 *Ibid.*, p. 197.

41 See Quine, *'Ontological Relativity' and Other Essays*.

42 Davidson, *Inquiries into Truth and Interpretation*, p. 279.

43 *Ibid.*, p. 280.

44 *Ibid.*, p. 229.

45 *Ibid.*, p. 225.

46 *Ibid.*, p. 162.

47 *Ibid.*, p. 197.

48 *Ibid.*, p. 197.

49 See Hans-Georg Gadamer, *Truth and Method*, trans. John Cumming and Garrett Barden (London: Sheed & Ward, 1979) and *Philosophical*

Hermeneutics, trans. David E. Linge (Berkeley & Los Angeles: University of California Press, 1977).

50 See especially Jürgen Habermas, 'Review of Gadamer's *Truth and Method*', in Thomas McCarthy and Fred Dallmayr (eds), *Understanding and Social Inquiry* (South Bend: Notre Dame, 1977). See also Habermas, *Knowledge and Human Interests*, trans. Jeremy J. Shapiro (London: Heinemann, 1972); *The Theory of Communicative Action*, Vol. 1 *(Reason and the Rationalization of Society)* and Vol. 2 *(Lifeworld and System: a critique of functionalist reason)*, both trans. Thomas McCarthy (Cambridge: Polity Press, 1987 and 1991). There is some useful commentary to be found in Hugh J. Silverman (ed.), *Gadamer and Hermeneutics* (London: Routledge, 1991).

51 See Peter Winch, *The Idea of a Social Science and its Relation to Philosophy* (London: Routledge & Kegan Paul, 1958); also *Trying to Explain* (Oxford: Basil Blackwell, 1987).

52 See details in note 50, above.

53 See Norris, *The Truth About Postmodernism*; also 'Deconstruction, Postmodernism and Philosophy: Habermas on Derrida', in Norris, *What's Wrong with Postmodernism: critical theory and the ends of philosophy* (Hemel Hempstead: Harvester-Wheatsheaf, 1990), pp. 49–76.

54 Onora O'Neill, *Constructions of Reason: explorations of Kant's practical philosophy* (Cambridge: Cambridge University Press, 1989).

55 *Ibid.*, p. 16.

56 See Hans Reiss (ed.), *Kant's Political Writings* (Cambridge: Cambridge University Press, 1970) and L. W. Beck, R. E. Anchor and E. L. Fackenham (eds), *Kant: on history* (Indianapolis: Bobbs-Merrill, 1963).

57 Akbar S. Ahmed, *Postmodernism and Islam: predicament and promise* (London: Routledge, 1992).

58 See Winch, *The Idea of a Social Science*.

59 O'Neill, *Constructions of Reason*, p. 171.

60 Mary Midgley, 'On Trying Out One's New Sword', in *Heart and Mind: the varieties of moral experience* (Brighton: Harvester, 1981), pp. 69–75.

61 Alasdair MacIntyre offered some of the sharpest criticisms of this way of thinking before he came around to his own (Aristotelian) version of the 'forms of life' argument. See MacIntyre, *Against the Self-Images of the Age* (London: Duckworth, 1971); also Martin Hollis and Steven Lukes (eds), *Rationality and Relativism* (Oxford: Basil Blackwell, 1982).

62 O'Neill, *Constructions of Reason*, p. 168.

63 *Ibid.*, p. 174.

64 *Ibid.*, p. 174.

65 See MacIntyre; also Donald Davidson, *Essays on Actions and Events* (Oxford: Clarendon Press, 1980).

66 O'Neill, *Constructions of Reason*, p. 180.

67 *Ibid.*, p. 25.

68 Lyotard, *The Postmodern Condition*; Peter Gay, *The Enlightenment: an interpretation*, 2 vols (London: Weidenfeld & Nicolson, 1967 and 1970).

69 Lyotard, *ibid.*, p. 82.

70 See Boyne, *Foucault and Derrida*; also Norris, ' "What Is Enlightenment?": Foucault on Kant', in *The Truth About Postmodernism*, pp. 29–99, and Richard Wolin, 'Foucault's Aesthetic Decisionism', *Telos*, No. 67 (1986).

71 Derrida, 'Cogito and the History of Madness', p. 55.

72 *Ibid.*, p. 74.

73 Rodolphe Gasché, *The Tain of the Mirror: Derrida and the philosophy of reflection* (Cambridge, Mass.: Harvard University Press, 1986).

74 See for instance Nancy Fraser, 'Foucault on Modern Power: empirical insights and normative confusions', *Praxis International*, Vol. 1 (1981), pp. 272–87; also Lois McNay, *Foucault and Feminism: power, gender and the self* (Cambridge: Polity Press, 1992); D.C. Hoy (ed.), *Foucault: a critical reader* (Oxford: Blackwell, 1986); and Peter Burke (ed.), *Critical Essays on Michel Foucault* (London: Scolar Press, 1992).

75 For criticism of this and other aspects of post-structuralist thinking, see for instance Perry Anderson, *In the Tracks of Historical Materialism* (London: Verso, 1983); Christopher Norris, *The Contest of Faculties: philosophy and theory after deconstruction* (London: Methuen, 1985) and *Deconstruction and the Interests of Theory* (London: Pinter Publishers, 1988); Raymomnd Tallis, *Not Saussure* (London: Macmillan, 1988); Valentine Cunningham, *In the Reading Gaol: postmodernity, texts and history* (Oxford: Basil Blackwell, 1994).

76 See especially Emmanuel Levinas, *Totality and Infinity*, trans. A. Lingis (Pittsburgh: Duquesne University Press, 1969).

77 See Lyotard, *The Postmodern Condition*; also Arkady Plotnitsky, *In the Shadow of Hegel: complementarity, history, and the unconscious* (Gainesville, Fl: University Press of Florida, 1993).

78 For a variety of critical perspectives on this issue, see Dieter Freundlieb and Wayne Hudson (eds), *Reason and its Other* (Providence, RI & Oxford: Berg Publishers, 1993); also – among the more influential source-texts – Michel de Certeau, *Heterologies: discourse on the other*, trans. Brian Massumi (Manchester: Manchester University Press, 1986).

79 See especially Jean-François Lyotard and Jean-Loup Thébaud, *Just Gaming*, trans. Wlad Godzich (Manchester: Manchester University Press, 1986).

80 Clifford Geertz, *Local Knowledge*; also *The Interpretation of Culture: selected essays* (New York: Basic Books, 1973) and *Works and Lives: the anthropologist as author* (Cambridge: Polity Press, 1988).

81 This debate receives its most elaborate theoretical treatment in John Guillory, *Cultural Capital: the problem of literary canon formation* (Chicago: University of Chicago Press, 1993).

82 See especially Geertz, 'Blurred Genres: the refiguration of social thought', in *Local Knowledge*, pp. 19–35.

83 See Derrida, 'From Restricted to General Economy: a Hegelianism without reserve', in *Writing and Difference*, pp. 251–77.

84 See for instance Roland Barthes, 'The Death of the Author', in *Image–Music–Text*, ed. and trans. Stephen Heath (London: Fontana, 1977), pp. 142–8; *Roland Barthes by Roland Barthes*, trans. Richard Howard (London: Macmillan, 1977); Michel Foucault, *The Order of Things: an archaeology of the human sciences* (New York: Random House, 1973); Sean Burke, *The Death and Return of the Author: criticism and subjectivity in Barthes, Foucault and Derrida* (Edinburgh: Edinburgh University Press, 1992); Eduardo Cadava, Peter Connor and Jean-Luc Nancy (eds), *Who Comes After the Subject?* (New York and London: Routledge, 1991).

85 Norris, ' "What Is Enlightenment?": Foucault on Kant', in *The Truth About Postmodernism*.

86 Gilbert Ryle, *The Concept of Mind* (London: Hutchinson, 1949).

87 See especially Foucault, *The Order of Things*.

88 See Fraser, 'Foucault on Modern Power'; also Michael Walzer, 'The Politics of Michel Foucault', in Hoy (ed.), *Foucault: a critical reader*, pp. 51–68.

89 Habermas, *The Philosophical Discourse of Modernity*.

90 Derrida, 'Cogito and the History of Madness', pp. 54–5.

91 Foucault, *Folie et déraison*, 2nd edn (Paris: Gallimard, 1972). The Appendix (including his response to Derrida) appears under the title 'My Body, this Paper, this Fire', trans. Geoffrey Bennington, *The Oxford Literary Review*, Vol. IV, No. 1 (1979), pp. 5–28.

92 Derrida, 'Cogito and the History of Madness', p. 54.

93 *Ibid.*, pp. 60–1.

94 Derrida, 'Violence and Metaphysics: an essay on the thought of Emmanuel Levinas', in *Writing and Difference*, pp. 79–153.

95 See for instance Derrida, 'The Principle of Reason' and 'Of an Apocalyptic Tone Recently Adopted in Philosophy', in Peter D. Fenves (ed.), *On the Rise of Tone in Philosophy: Kant and Derrida* (Baltimore: Johns Hopkins University Press, 1992).

96 Levinas, *Totality and Infinity*.

97 Derrida, 'Violence and Metaphysics', p. 123.

98 Cited by Derrida, *ibid.*, p. 125.

99 Simon Critchley, *The Ethics of Deconstruction: Derrida and Levinas* (Oxford: Basil Blackwell, 1992). See also Robert Bernasconi and Simon Critchley (eds), *Re-Reading Levinas* (London: Athlone Press, 1991).

100 Derrida, 'Violence and Metaphysics', p. 123.

101 *Ibid.*, p. 123.

102 *Ibid.*, p. 152.

103 *Ibid.*, p. 151.

104 Derrida, 'At This Very Moment in This Work Here I am', trans. Ruben Berezdivin, in Robert Bernasconi and Simon Critchley (eds), *Re-Reading Levinas*.

105 Derrida, 'Violence and Metaphysics', p. 151.

106 See for instance Edward Said, *Orientalism* (New York: Vintage Books, 1979) and *Covering Islam: how the media and the experts determine how we see the rest of the world* (London: Routledge, 1981); also – for a different but related critical perspective – François Hartog, *The Mirror of Herodotus: the representation of the other in the writing of history* (Berkeley & Los Angeles: University of California Press, 1988).

107 Stephen Greenblatt, 'Invisible Bullets: Renaissance authority and its subversion', *Glyph,* Vol. VIII (1981), pp. 40–60. See also Greenblatt, *Renaissance Self-Fashioning: from More to Shakespeare* (Chicago: University of Chicago Press, 1980); *Shakespearean Negotiations: the circulation of social energy in Renaissance England* (Oxford: Clarendon Press, 1988); *Learning to Curse: essays in early modern culture* (London: Routledge, 1990); Greenblatt (ed.), *Representing the English Renaissance* (Berkeley & Los Angeles: University of California Press, 1988); and Richard Wilson and Richard Dutton (eds), *New Historicism and Renaissance Drama* (London: Longman, 1992).

108 Many of these criticisms are to be found clearly formulated in Emile Benveniste, *Problems in General Linguistics,* trans. Mary E. Meek (Coral Gables: University of Miami Press, 1971).

109 As argued by (e.g.) Tallis, *Not Saussure,* Norris, *Uncritical Theory,* and Cunningham, *In the Reading Gaol.*

110 See for instance Lyotard, *The Differend* and *The Inhuman: reflections on time,* trans. Geoffrey Bennington and Rachel Bowlby (Cambridge: Polity Press, 1991).

111 For a useful corrective see Salim Kemal, *Kant and Fine Art: an essay on Kant and the philosophy of fine art and culture* (Oxford: Clarendon Press, 1986).

112 Said, *Orientalism* and *Covering Islam.*

113 For a more extended treatment of this intellectual history, see Christopher Norris, *Spinoza and the Origins of Modern Critical Theory* (Oxford: Basil Blackwell, 1991).

114 See Lyotard, *The Postmodern Condition,* p. 179.

115 See Norris, 'Kant Disfigured: ethics, deconstruction and the post-modern sublime', in *The Truth About Postmodernism*, pp. 182–256.

116 For some alternative (and better informed) accounts to set against this current postmodernist wisdom, see Peter Dews, *Logics of Disintegration: post-structuralist thought and the claims of theory* (London: Verso, 1987); Terry Eagleton, *The Ideology of the Aesthetic* (Oxford: Basil Blackwell, 1990); Manfred Frank, *What Is Neo-Structuralism?* (Minneapolis: University of Minnesota Press, 1990); Andrew Bowie, *Aesthetics and Subjectivity from Kant to Nietzsche* (Manchester: Manchester University Press, 1990); Gillian Rose, *Dialectic of Nihilism: post-structuralism and law* (Oxford: Basil Blackwell, 1980).

117 Norris, *Uncritical Theory*.

118 Francis Fukuyama, 'Changed Days for Ruritania's Dictator', *The Guardian*, 8 April 1991, p. 19. See also Fukuyama, *The End of History and the Last Man* (London: Hamish Hamilton, 1992).

119 For some oblique reflections in this 'life-and-work' mode, see Geoffrey Bennington and Jacques Derrida, *Jacques Derrida*, trans. Geoffrey Bennington (Chicago: University of Chicago Press, 1983).

120 Derrida, 'Violence and Metaphysics', p. 125.

121 *Ibid.*, p. 151.

122 See Derrida, *'Speech and Phenomena' and Other Essays on Husserl's Theory of Signs*, trans. David B. Allison (Evanston, Ill.: Northwestern University Press, 1973); *Of Grammatology*, trans. Gayatri Chakravorty Spivak (Baltimore: Johns Hopkins University Press, 1976); 'Plato's Pharmacy', in *Dissemination*, trans. Barbara Johnson (London: Athlone Press, 1981), pp. 61–171.

123 Derrida, 'Violence and Metaphysics', p. 153.

124 Matthew Arnold, *Culture and Anarchy*, in *Culture and Anarchy and other writings*, ed. Stephan Collini (Cambridge: Cambridge University Press, 1993), pp. 53–187; pp. 126–7.

125 Derrida, 'Violence and Metaphysics', p. 97.

126 Derrida, 'Cogito and the History of Madness', p. 56.

127 *Ibid.*, p. 62.

128 Derrida, 'Violence and Metaphysics', p. 151.

129 See Derrida, *Speech and Phenomena*; also *Edmund Husserl's 'Origin of Geometry': an introduction*, trans. John P. Leavey (Pittsburgh: Duquesne University Press, 1978).

130 Derrida, ' "Genesis and Structure" and Phenomenology', in *Writing and Difference*, pp. 154–68; p. 160.

131 *Ibid.*, p. 158.

132 Derrida, 'Violence and Metaphysics', p. 153.

133 Derrida, 'The Supplement of Copula: philosophy before linguistics', in *Margins of Philosophy*, trans. Alan Bass (Chicago: University of Chicago Press, 1982), pp. 175–205.

134 Emile Benveniste, *Problems in General Linguistics*, trans. Mary E. Meek (Coral Gables: University of Miami Press, 1971).

135 Derrida, 'The Supplement of Copula', p. 192.

136 The text to which Benveniste and Derrida mainly refer is Aristotle's discussion of the categories in *Metaphysics*, Chapter 6, trans. Hugh Tredenick (Cambridge, Mass.: Harvard University Press, 1933), p. 299. See also Aristotle, *Categories and De Interpretatione*, ed. & trans. J. L. Ackrill (Oxford: Clarendon Press, 1963) and the section on the categories of judgment in Kant, *Critique of Pure Reason*, trans. N. Kemp Smith (New York: St Martin's Press, 1965), pp. 113–4.

137 Derrida, 'The Supplement of Copula', p. 192.

138 *Ibid.*, p. 180.

139 *Ibid.*, p. 180.

140 Benjamin Lee Whorf, *Language, Thought and Reality: selected writings*, ed J. B. Carroll (Cambridge, Mass.: MIT Press, 1956).

141 Derrida, 'The Supplement of Copula', p. 184.

142 Benveniste, *Problems in General Linguistics*, p. 62.

143 Derrida, 'The Supplement of Copula', p. 198.

144 *Ibid.*, p. 201.

145 *Ibid.*, p. 197.

146 *Ibid.*, p. 199.

147 *Ibid.*, p. 199.

148 Edward Said, *Culture and Imperialism* (London: Chatto & Windus, 1993), p. 21.

149 C. L. R. James, *The Black Jacobins: Toussaint l'Ouverture and the San Domingo revolution* (New York: Random House, 1963).

150 Said, *Culture and Imperialism*, p. 338.

151 Said, *Orientalism* and *Covering Islam*; *The World, the Text, and the Critic* (Cambridge, Mass.: Harvard University Press, 1983).

152 See Said, *The World, the Text, and the Critic*.

153 See Stanley Fish, *Doing What Comes Naturally: change, rhetoric, and the practice of theory in literary and legal studies* (Oxford: Clarendon Press, 1989); also Fish, 'Commentary: the young and restless', in H. Aram Veeser (ed.), *The New Historicism* (New York and London: Routledge, 1989), pp. 303–16.

154 Stephen Greenblatt, 'Invisible Bullets: Renaissance authority and its subversion', *Glyph*, Vol. VIII (1981), pp. 40–60.

155 For some vigorous argument to this effect, see Cunningham, *In the Reading Gaol*.

156 Elizabeth Fox-Genovese, 'Literary Criticism and the Politics of the New Historicism', in Veeser, *The New Historicism*, pp. 213–2. Other contributors to this volume (among them Catherine Gallagher, Gerald Graff, and Frank Lentricchia) likewise have criticisms to offer on methodological and political grounds. See also Brook Thomas, *The*

New Historicism, and other old-fashioned topics (Princeton, NJ: Princeton University Press, 1991) and Arnaldo Momigliano, *Studies in Historiography* (London: Weidenfeld & Nicolson, 1966).

157 T. S. Eliot, 'Tradition and the Individual Talent', in *Selected Essays* (London: Faber, 1964), pp. 3–11; also Eliot, *Knowledge and Experience in the Philosophy of F. H. Bradley* (London: Faber, 1964).

158 See especially Foucault, *Language, Counter-Memory, Practice*, trans. Donald F. Bouchard and S. Simon (Oxford: Basil Blackwell, 1977).

159 Habermas, *The Philosophical Discourse of Modernity*.

160 For an informative survey of these developments in post-Kantian intellectual history, see Frederick C. Beiser, *The Fate of Reason: German philosophy from Kant to Fichte* and *Enlightenment, Revolution, and Romanticism: the genesis of modern German political thought* (Cambridge, Mass.: Harvard University Press, 1987 and 1992).

161 Manfred Frank, *What Is Neo-Structuralism?* (op. cit.).

162 Habermas, *The New Conservatism: cultural criticism and the historians' debate*, ed. & trans. Shierry Weber (Cambridge: Polity Press, 1989). See also Peter Dews (ed.), *Habermas, Autonomy and Solidarity: interviews with Jürgen Habermas* (London: Verso, 1986) and Robert C. Holub, *Jürgen Habermas: critic in the public sphere* (London: Routledge, 1991).

163 Rorty, 'Nineteenth-Century Idealism and Twentieth-Century Textualism', in *Consequences of Pragmatism*, pp. 139–59.

164 For a polemical but none the less cogent critique of these ideas, see Terry Eagleton, *Ideology: an introduction* (London: Verso, 1991).

165 Julia Kristeva, *Strangers to Ourselves*, trans. Leon S. Roudiez (Hemel Hempstead: Harvester-Wheatsheaf, 1991) and *Nations Without Nationalism*, trans. Roudiez (New York: Columbia University Press, 1993).

166 Kristeva, *The Revolution in Poetic Language*, trans. Margaret Waller (New York: Columbia University Press, 1984). See also Kristeva, *Desire in Language: a semiotic approach to literature and art*, trans. Leon S. Roudiez (Oxford: Basil Blackwell, 1980); *Language, the Unknown: an initiation into linguistics*, trans. Anne M. Menke (Hemel Hempstead: Harvester-Wheatsheaf, 1989); Toril Moi (ed.), *The Kristeva Reader* (Oxford: Basil Blackwell, 1986).

167 See Roland Barthes, *S/Z*, trans. Richard Miller (London: Jonathan Cape, 1975); also Philippe Sollers, *Writing and the Experience of Limits*, ed. David Hayman, trans. Philip Barnard and David Hayman (New York: Columbia University Press, 1983).

168 For a more sympathetic account of these ideas, see John Mowitt, *Text: the genealogy of an antidisciplinary object* (Durham, NC: Duke University Press, 1993); also Michael Payne, 'Revolution in Poetic Language', in *Reading Theory: an introduction to Lacan, Derrida and*

Kristeva (Oxford: Basil Blackwell, 1993), pp. 162–211 and Philip E. Lewis, 'Revolutionary Semiotics', *Diacritics,* Vol. IV, No. 3 (Fall 1974), pp. 28–32.

169 See Geert Lernout, *The French Joyce* (Ann Arbor: University of Michigan Press, 1990).

170 See for instance Kristeva, *Powers of Horror: an essay on abjection, Tales of Love* and *Black Sun: depression and melancholia,* all trans. Leon S. Roudiez (New York: Columbia University Press, 1982, 1987 and 1989).

171 See Kristeva, *Revolution in Poetic Language* and *Powers of Horror.*

172 Jean-François Lyotard, *Libidinal Economy,* trans. Ian Hamilton Grant (London: Athlone Press, 1993).

173 Terry Eagleton, 'It is not quite true that I have a body, and not quite true that I am one either' (review of *Body Works* by Peter Brooks), *The London Review of Books,* Vol. XV, No. 10 (27 May 1993), pp. 7–8. See also Eagleton, *The Ideology of the Aesthetic.*

174 See for instance Michèle Le Doeuff, *The Philosophical Imaginary,* trans. Colin Gordon (London: Athlone Press, 1989) and *Hipparchia's Choice: an essay concerning women,* trans. Trista Selous (Oxford: Basil Blackwell, 1991); also Genevieve Lloyd, *The Man of Reason: 'male' and 'female' in Western philosophy* (London: Methuen, 1984); Andrea Nye, *Feminist Theory and the Philosophies of Man* (London: Croom Helm, 1988) and *Words of Power: a feminist reading of the history of logic* (London: Routledge, 1990).

175 See Mary Jacobus, 'Reading Woman (Reading)' and 'The Difference of View', in *Reading Woman: essays in feminist criticism* (New York: Columbia University Press, 1986), pp. 3–24 & 27–40; Alice Jardine and Paul Smith (eds), *Men in Feminism* (London: Methuen, 1987); Elaine Showalter, 'Critical Cross-Dressing', *Raritan,* Vol. III, No. 2 (Fall 1983), pp. 130–49.

176 Derrida, *Spurs: Nietzsche's styles,* trans. Barbara Harlow (Chicago: University of Chicago Press, 1979).

177 Paul de Man, 'Crisis and Criticism', in *Blindness and Insight: essays in the rhetoric of contemporary criticism* (London: Methuen, 1983), pp. 3–19.

178 Edmund Husserl, *The Crisis of European Sciences and Transcendental Phenomenology,* trans. D. Carr (Evanston, Ill.: Northwestern University Press, 1970).

179 de Man, 'Crisis and Criticism', p. 15.

180 *Ibid.,* p. 15.

181 *Ibid.,* p. 16.

182 *Ibid.,* p. 16.

183 *Ibid.,* p. 16.

184 *Ibid.,* p. 15.

185 Kristeva, *Strangers to Ourselves*, p. 1.
186 *Ibid.*, p. 191.
187 Cited by Kristeva, *ibid.*, p. 120.
188 *Ibid.*, p. 120.
189 See for instance David Miller, *Philosophy and Ideology in Hume's Political Thought* (Oxford: Clarendon Press, 1981).
190 Michel de Montaigne, 'On Cannibals', in *The Complete Works of Montaigne*, trans. Donald M. Frame (London: Hamilton, 1958), pp. 150–8.
191 William Empson, *Some Version of Pastoral* (Penguin: Harmondsworth, 1966), p. 22. I attempt to fill out the philosophical background of this and similar remarks in 'For Truth in Criticism: Empson and the claims of theory', Norris, *The Truth About Postmodernism*, pp. 100–81 and 'Empson as Literary Theorist: from Ambiguity to Complex Words and beyond', in Christopher Norris and Nigel Mapp (eds.), *William Empson: the critical achievement* (Cambridge: Cambridge University Press, 1993), pp. 1–120.
192 Kristeva, *Strangers to Ourselves*, p. 122.
193 *Ibid.*, pp. 122–3.
194 See for instance Charles Taylor, *Sources of the Self: the making of the modern identity* (Cambridge: Cambridge University Press, 1989) and Anthony J. Cascardi, *The Subject of Modernity* (Cambridge: Cambridge University Press, 1992).
195 Kristeva, *Strangers to Ourselves*, p. 29.
196 *Ibid.*, p. 190.
197 *Ibid.*, p. 153.
198 *Ibid.*, p. 152.
199 John Rawls, 'Kantian Constructivism in Moral Theory', *The Journal of Philosophy*, Vol. LXXVII, No. 9 (September 1980), pp. 515–72; 'Justice as Fairness: political not metaphysical', *Philosophy and Public Affairs*, Vol. XIV (1985), pp. 223–51.
200 Rawls, *A Theory of Justice* (Oxford: Clarendon Press, 1972).
201 Rawls, 'Justice as Fairness', p. 224.
202 *Ibid.*, p. 233.
203 *Ibid.*, p. 234.
204 See for instance Michael Walzer, *Spheres of Justice: a defence of pluralism and equality* (Oxford: Basil Blackwell, 1983) and *Interpretation and Social Criticism* (Cambridge, Mass.: Harvard University Press, 1987); also Michael Sandel, *Liberalism and the Limits of Justice* (Cambridge: Cambridge University Press, 1982).
205 Rawls, 'Kantian Constructivism', p. 532.
206 *Ibid.*, p. 532.
207 Robert Nozick, *Anarchy, State and Utopia* (Oxford: Basil Blackwell, 1974).

208 Rawls, 'Justice as Fairness', p. 241.
209 See for instance Rorty, *Contingency, Irony, and Solidarity* (op. cit.).
210 For a representative sampling see Cadava, Connor and Nancy (eds), *Who Comes After the Subject?*.
211 Richard Rorty, 'Moral Identity and Private Autonomy: the case of Foucault', in *Essays on Heidegger and Others* (Cambridge: Cambridge University Press, 1991), pp. 193–8.
212 See especially Foucault, *Language, Counter-Memory, Practice* and *Power/Knowledge: selected interviews and other writings* (Brighton: Harvester, 1980).
213 Rawls, 'Justice as Fairness', p. 244.
214 *Ibid.*, p. 244.
215 Montesquieu, *The Spirit of the Laws,* trans. and ed. A. M. Cohler, B. C. Miller and H. S. Stone (Cambridge: Cambridge University Press, 1989).
216 Kristeva, *Strangers to Ourselves*, p. 152.
217 *Ibid.*, p. 153.
218 Lyotard, *The Differend.*
219 Max Horkheimer and Theodor W. Adorno, *Dialectic of Enlightenment* (London: Verso, 1979); also Adorno, *Negative Dialectics,* trans. E. B. Ashton (London: Routledge, 1973) and *Minima Moralia: reflections from a damaged life,* trans. E. F. N. Jephcott (London: New Left Books, 1974).
220 See for instance Julia Kristeva, *The Revolution in Poetic Language* and 'Word, Dialogue, and Novel', in Moi (ed.), *The Kristeva Reader*, pp. 34–61.
221 Fish, *Doing What Comes Naturally.*
222 See Aristotle, *Nicomachean Ethics,* trans. J. L. Ackrill (London: Faber, 1973), especially Chapter 6; also *The Art of Rhetoric,* trans. John Henry Freese (London: Heinemann, 1926).
223 See for instance Stuart Hampshire, *Thought and Action* (London: Chatto & Windus, 1959) and *Morality and Conflict* (Oxford: Basil Blackwell, 1983).
224 The best-known statement of this emotivist position is C. L. Stevenson, *Ethics and Language* (New Haven: Yale University Press, 1944). See also William Empson's critique of such thinking – argued from a logico-semantic and rational–humanist standpoint – in *The Structure of Complex Words,* pp. 414–29.
225 Kristeva, *Strangers to Ourselves*, pp. 172–3.
226 *Ibid.*, p. 227.
227 Cited by Kristeva, *Ibid.*, p. 130.
228 *Ibid.*, p. 195.
229 Derrida, 'The Laws of Reflection: Nelson Mandela, in admiration', trans. Mary Ann Caws and Isabelle Lorenz, in Jacques Derrida and

Mustapha Tlili (eds), *For Nelson Mandela* (New York: Henry Holt & Co., 1987), pp. 13–42.

230 Derrida, 'Racism's Last Word', trans. Peggy Kamuf, *Critical Inquiry*, Vol. XII (1985), pp. 290–9. Among the responses to this essay, see Anne McClintock and Rob Nixon, 'No Names Apart: the separation of word and history in Derrida's "Le dernier mot du racisme', *Critical Inquiry*, Vol. XIII (1986), pp. 140–54; also Derrida, 'But beyond . . . (Open Letter to Anne McClintock and Rob Nixon)', *Critical Inquiry*, Vol. XIII (1986), pp. 155–70.

231 For further reflection on this topic, see David Dyzenhaus, *Hard Cases in Wicked Legal Systems: South African law in the perspective of legal philosophy* (Oxford: Clarendon Press, 1991).

232 Kristeva, *Strangers to Ourselves*, p. 153.

233 *Ibid.*, p. 153.

234 *Ibid.*, p. 129.

235 Lyotard, *The Differend*, p. 179.

236 Cited by Kristeva, *Strangers to Ourselves*, pp. 129–30.

237 *Ibid.*, p. 129.

238 Elizabeth Fox-Genovese, 'Literary Criticism and the Politics of the New Historicism', in Veeser (ed.), *The New Historicism*, pp. 213–24; p. 216; also Hayden White, *Tropics of Discourse: essays in cultural criticism* and *The Content of the Form* (Baltimore: Johns Hopkins University Press, 1978 and 1988); Robert Hodge, *Literature as Discourse: textual strategies in English and history* (Baltimore: Johns Hopkins University Press, 1990).

239 Said, *Culture and Imperialism*, p. 368.

240 *Ibid.*, p. 368.

241 See Norris, *Spinoza and the Origins of Modern Critical Theory*.

242 Akbar Ahmed, *Postmodernism and Islam: predicament and promise* (London: Routledge, 1992).

243 Said, *Culture and Imperialism*, p. 368.

244 *Ibid.*, p. 368.

245 Norris, *Spinoza*.

246 See William Empson, *Milton's God* (London: Chatto & Windus, 1961).

247 See especially W. K. Wimsatt, *The Verbal Icon: studies in the meaning of poetry* (Lexington, Ky: University of Kentucky Press, 1954).

248 Wimsatt, *The Day of the Leopards: essays in defense of poems* (New Haven: Yale University Press, 1976).

249 Perry Anderson, *A Zone of Engagement* (London: Verso, 1992).

250 Andreas Hillgruber, *Europa in der Weltpolitik der Nachkriegszeit* (Munich: Oldenbourg, 1989).

251 Lyotard, *The Differend*, pp. 3–4, 14–16, 18–9, 32–3.

252 Norris, *What's Wrong with Postmodernism* and *Uncritical Theory*.

253 Anderson, *Zones of Engagement*, p. 180.

254 See Linda Hutcheon, *A Poetics of Postmodernism: history, theory, fiction* (London: Routledge, 1988) and *The Politics of Postmodernism* (London: Routledge, 1989).

255 Simon Schama, *Dead Certainties* (London: Faber, 1991).

256 See for instance Jerome S. Bruner, *Actual Minds, Possible Worlds* (Cambridge, Mass.: Harvard University Press, 1986); David Lewis, *On the Plurality of Worlds* (Oxford: Basil Blackwell, 1986); Brian McHale, *Postmodernist Fiction* (London: Methuen, 1987); Thomas Pavel, *Fictional Worlds* (Cambridge, Mass.: Harvard University Press, 1987).

257 Terry Lovell, *Pictures of Reality: aesthetics, politics and pleasure* (London: British Film Institute, 1980), p. 37. Cited in Michèle Barrett, *The Politics of Truth: from Marx to Foucault* (Cambridge: Polity Press, 1991).

258 See also Terry Eagleton, 'Discourse and Ideology', in *Ideology: an introduction*, pp. 193–220.

259 Carolyn Porter, 'History and Literature: "After the New Historicism"', *New Literary History*, Winter 1990, pp. 253–72; p. 261.

260 Michel Foucault, *Les mots et les choses* (Paris: Gallimard, 1966); English title *The Order of Things: an archaeology of the human sciences* (New York: Pantheon, 1970). See also Foucault, *The Archaeology of Knowledge*, trans. A. Sheridan-Smith (New York: Harper & Row, 1972).

261 Foucault, *The Birth of the Clinic*, trans. A. Sheridan-Smith (London: Tavistock, 1973); *Madness and Civilization: a history of insanity in the age of reason*, trans. Richard Howard (London: Tavistock, 1971); *Discipline and Punish: the birth of the prison*, trans. A. Sheridan-Smith (New York: Pantheon, 1973).

262 See especially the essays collected in Foucault, *Language, Counter-Memory, Practice*, trans. & ed. Donald F. Bouchard and Sherry Simon (Ithaca: Cornell University Press, 1977); also *Power/Knowledge: selected interviews and other writings* (Brighton: Harvester, 1980) and *Politics, Philosophy, Culture*, ed. Laurence D. Kritzman (New York: Routledge, 1988).

263 Foucault, *The History of Sexuality*, Vol. 1, *An Introduction*, trans. Robert Hurley (Harmondsworth: Penguin, 1981).

264 Foucault, *The Use of Pleasure*, trans. R. Hurley (Harmondsworth: Penguin, 1986) and *The Care of the Self*, trans. Hurley (New York: Random House, 1986). See also the essays and interviews collected in *The Final Foucault*, ed. J. Bernauer and D. Rasmussen (Cambridge, Mass.: MIT Press, 1988).

265 Foucault, interview with Paul Rabinow, in *The Foucault Reader*, ed. Rabinow (Penguin: Harmondsworth, 1986), pp. 381–90, p. 381.

266 Foucault, 'What Is Enlightenment?' in *The Foucault Reader*, pp. 32–50. See also Immanuel Kant, 'What Is Enlightenment?', in *Kant's Political Writings*, ed. Hans Reiss (Cambridge: Cambridge University Press, 1966); Jürgen Habermas, 'Taking Aim at the Heart of the Present', in D. C. Hoy (ed.), *Foucault: a critical reader* (Oxford: Basil Blackwell, 1986), pp. 103–8; and Hubert Dreyfus and Paul Rabinow, 'What Is Maturity?: Habermas and Foucault on "What Is Enlightenment?" ', *ibid.*, pp. 109–21.

267 Foucault, 'What Is Enlightenment?', p. 49.

268 *Ibid.*, p. 46.

269 See for instance Richard Rorty, *Contingency, Irony, and Solidarity* (Cambridge: Cambridge University Press, 1989) and 'Moral Identity and Private Autonomy: the case of Foucault', *Essays on Heidegger and Others* (Cambridge: Cambridge University Press, 1991), pp. 193–98.

270 Foucault, 'What Is Enlightenment?', p. 42.

271 Foucault, interview with Rabinow, p. 388.

272 *Ibid.*, p. 390.

273 Foucault, 'Politics and Ethics' (an interview), in *The Foucault Reader*, pp. 371–80; p. 376.

Index of names